Rock Island Public Library
401 - 19th Street
Rock Island, IL 61201-8143

We Are All From Uranus

We Are All From Uranus

*How to Have
Out-of-This-World
Relationships*

Rebecca Lane

and

Charles E. Bailey, M.D.

GIST PUBLISHING • LAKE MARY, FLORIDA

We Are All From Uranus: How to Have Out-of-This-World Relationships

Copyright © 2013 by Rebecca Lane and Charles E. Bailey, M.D.

All rights reserved. No part of this book may be reproduced or transmitted in any form or by any means, electronic or mechanical, including photocopying, recording, or by any information storage or retrieval system, without permission in writing of both the copyright owner and the publisher of this book. Profits from this book to be donated to the Global Institute for Scientific Thinking, a tax-exempt nonprofit organization.

All information provided is believed and intended to be reliable, but accuracy is not guaranteed by the publisher.

Opinions expressed are those of the authors and *should not* be construed as individual professional advice. The reader *should* evaluate available resources and consult with a professional counselor.

Published in the United States of America by
GIST Publishing Company, Inc.
Lake Mary, Florida
www.gistinc.org/gistpub.html

ISBN: 978-1-936264-23-0 softcover
       978-1-936264-24-7 ebook

LCCN: 2013939254

Copyediting: Katharine O'Moore-Klopf, ELS, of KOK Edit;
    www.kokedit.com
Cover photo of Uranus: Heidi Hammel;
    Massachusetts Institute of Technology and NASA/ESA
Design and composition: Dick Margulis Creative Services;
    www.dmargulis.com
Proofreading: Sharyn Mathews, of Cat's Paw Studio

MANUFACTURED IN THE UNITED STATES OF AMERICA

Contents

	Prologue	vii
	Introduction	x
Chapter 1	I Love You. You're Perfect. Now Change!	3
Chapter 2	There's No Self-Acceptance on Uranus	20
Chapter 3	The *Should*-ectomy...	30
Chapter 4	Where Do Feelings Come From?	40
Chapter 5	Responsibility Versus Influence	57
Chapter 6	Is It Love, or What?	70
Chapter 7	The Wrath of Uranus	85
Chapter 8	The Thrill Is Gone	93
Chapter 9	Fine-Tuning Your Relationship Skills	105
Chapter 10	Advanced Training	119
Chapter 11	Fixing Your Partner and Others	130
Chapter 12	Alleged Codependency	147
Chapter 13	Epilogue	155
Appendix I	Quick Reference	160
Appendix II	Exercises	165
Appendix III	Recommended Reading	172

Prologue

The Beginning

THIS WAS IT. HE'D surprised her with a romantic dinner complete with candlelight and roses. As they slowly undressed each other, she could feel her euphoria rising with each drugging kiss, each searing caress. With every heated look, she felt beautiful, wanted, desired. The soft flickering light from the vanilla-scented candles cast a dreamy atmosphere, enhancing each soft touch and whispered endearment in the glowing half-light. She loved him. She could feel it in every fiber of her being. As he pulled back, looking at her with tenderness and longing, she knew he felt the same way; she saw it deep within his eyes. It wasn't just this intense physical connection, the sparks flying between them, but his tenderness—the way he listened to her every word, comforted her when she hurt. She felt a strong primal desire to do all that was in her power to make this strong, passionate, caring man as happy as he made her. As they came together, she knew without a doubt this was the man for her. The only man she wanted to be with, love, and cherish. Forever...

He couldn't get enough of her. He had planned this night with care, wanting to make her feel special, wanting to show her how intensely he desired and cherished her. The satiny feel of her skin begged for his touch. Her own unique scent tugged at him, telling him it was this woman that he wanted and loved, and that all others paled in her light. It was her smile, the look she had given him when he'd revealed the bedroom he'd transformed into a warm love nest, the soft sigh she made now as he kissed her neck. It was the way she cared and was there for him. He knew as he held her in his arms that she was the one he wanted and could not live without, the one he would love and cherish...forever....He was hers, just as she was his.

Their love was the stuff of legends. This princess and her prince would live happily ever after...forever, for eternity....And then the honeymoon period ended. No more roses and candlelight. No more surprise romantic dinners, whispered endearments, soft caresses. Where the hell did all the romance go?

Sure, things change. Reality intrudes on passion. Money goes toward diapers for the children and not playtime for the adults. Good behavior and a desire to please are replaced by bad moods, stress, sweat pants, and a five o'clock shadow. The person who inspired passion and happiness is gone, replaced by someone who seems to frustrate and infuriate. How did it happen? When and how did things begin to change? Does it *have to* happen? Is there any hope? The prince and princess got married, but less than 50% of couples live happily ever after.

Well, Unfortunately, We Are All From Uranus
And while sometimes it may well feel as though we are from different planets, it's not necessarily the differences between men and women that disrupt relationships. On Uranus, both men and women have lousy relationship skills. They both have been taught or have inadvertently learned, by observation and

innocent interaction, how to have relationships on Uranus—or at least how they understand they are *supposed* to. This results in most of their relationships failing miserably.

On Uranus as society evolved and as men and women emerged from caves, their primitive state of knowledge about relationships was passed down from generation to generation. The current unhealthy fundamentals of relating originated in the dark ages, ages characterized by superstitions; by extreme and irrational fear of and belief in magic, witchcraft, and fantastical creatures; by ignorance; and by countless absurd beliefs and fantasies about fairy-tale relationships. The people on Uranus unwittingly continue to use the primitive ways of relating that they inherited from childhood. Never questioning, they refuse to challenge or change those unhealthy beliefs, as their relationships aimlessly sputter and self-destruct.

By now you might have guessed that on Uranus, people deny the folly of their ways. They naively rationalize, justify, signify, dignify, and delude themselves on their way through relationships. They think they know everything there is to know about relationships. On Uranus everyone is a self-proclaimed relationship expert: neighbors, friends, family, hosts of television talk shows, movie stars…and the list goes on and on. They know it all, and if you don't believe it, just ask. But unfortunately, on Uranus they really don't know everything about relationships. And unaware, they continue to struggle.

So how do we find our way back to those longing looks and passionate lovemaking — our happily ever after? Luckily, you can read along and have fun learning why we are *all* flawed and fallible humans. You may even be lucky enough to pick up a few helpful relationship tips, so you can go from feeling like the nagging fishwife or the haranguing husband to a transformed partner who understands what it takes to have intimate relationships that are out of this world.

Introduction

LET'S FACE IT. ON Uranus the odds favor the self-destruction of most relationships. Why is relationship success so elusive? More often than not, marriages end in divorce, the dreaded *d*-word. That shatters many dreams and breaks many hearts, leaving behind despair and despondency. Talk about a confidence-killer.

Have you ever taken your relationship skills for granted? On Uranus, most people do. They believe that love will conquer all. Yeah, right. It *should* be so easy. How do unhealthy beliefs survive when these beliefs not only don't work well but actually wreak havoc? Unfortunately, we often refuse to consider what it takes to help make a relationship successful, what it takes to feel good about our relationships. People stop, all too often, with the assumption that love will keep them together. There once was a man who had bragged for years about his perfect relationship. Then one day, instead of "My relationship is perfect," it was suddenly "She left me!" When asked, "What happened—I thought you had the perfect relationship?" He replied, "Well, it was perfect...for me. I don't know what went wrong. We didn't really talk about it; she just up and left. I thought she loved me."

INTRODUCTION

Sometimes love is not enough. Good intentions may not be enough. Great sex or immense wealth may not be enough. All of these fall short when it comes to overcoming poor relationship skills.

Let's Look at Barbara and Paul's Relationship

Barbara is college educated. In her mid-twenties she met Paul. They went on an awkward first date, which turned into a second, third, fourth, and so on. Paul seemed like the perfect guy. He had a good career, a great personality, a body to die for, and many interests in common with her, such as their mutual and unusual love for skunks, a grossly misunderstood creature in their opinion. Thankfully, both were well liked by their in-laws, although Barbara sometimes felt that Paul's mother took a little too much pleasure in giving her homemaking advice or lectures on her duties as Paul's wife. But as time passed in the marriage, things changed. Paul began spending more time at work and less time with Barbara. His claims of being too busy, of having this meeting or that business lunch, increased. Of course, the claims also resulted in leaving him less time to share, as they had agreed he would do, in the care of the two children who had joined the picture. Paul seemed preoccupied and didn't listen and pay attention to Barbara as he had before. He promised to change but didn't.

Barbara's doubts about her husband, their love life, and her marriage began to keep her awake at night, pushing her to start keeping track of how often Paul initiated romantic sex. She began to feel angry, frustrated, distant, and depressed a good deal of the time. She began to feel like a giant brick wall was forming between them, and she started to notice an increase in arguments, which aroused her fear that she was becoming the nagging wife she had vowed not to become. With dread, Barbara finally realized one afternoon, "Oh my God, I'm turning into my nagging mother." Now the thought "If he really loved me, he would..." pops into her head frequently.

Suddenly her life, or at least parts of it, seems to resemble the daytime talk shows she used to sneer at, and the lovelorn story lines of country and western songs sound alarmingly familiar. Her topic of choice during lunches and time spent with her friends has started to revolve more and more around her struggle to reform her self-absorbed husband. Conversations with him have become confrontations and tend to be either one-sided complaint marathons or very short-lived. One of them usually either walks away or starts yelling. She is utterly miserable, hates it, and fears she is doomed to feel this way for eternity unless the SOB changes. She now constantly asks herself, "What happened to the man I fell in love with? How did it all go wrong? I thought he loved me. He says he does, but I don't believe him. If he really loved me, he wouldn't treat me this way."

Barbara could use this book! *We Are All From Uranus* was written to help all of us who have received our relationship training from Uranus and want to beat the dismal relationship odds—we want good relationship skills to take over when love and good intentions are not enough. Maintaining healthy relationships, from casual to intimate, is one of life's most demanding and challenging adventures. Would you like to know ways to successfully promote long-lasting and satisfying relationships? Would you like to know the skills that were banned from Uranus? Would you like to know the healthy rules that will help you beat the odds?

You might be thinking, "You make it sound so easy." Feeling good about relationships is not easy, because it takes work to learn the skills so that they can work for you. The concepts are quite *simple*. However, they are not *easy* to put into practice. It takes significant effort to rid ourselves of unhealthy habits we have practiced for a long time. Whether the habits were

INTRODUCTION   xiii

accidentally and unwittingly learned or were passed down for generations as "truths of the universe," they create misery and agony and almost ensure dismal failures in relationships. Thus, this book can be a valuable tool. It may even eventually save you thousands of dollars in attorney's fees, along with the heartbreak that comes with them.

Rest assured that as you read and practice the principles in this book, you'll quickly realize benefits. *We Are All From Uranus* teaches you not only how to have better relationships with others but perhaps more important, how to have a good relationship with yourself. It helps to know how to love and take care of yourself if you want to spread that love to others.

Let's be clear. This book was written for people don't know it all. It even shows how to enlist partners, even unwilling ones, to maximize relationship outcomes and to feel good about relationships again.

One final word: There are a bazillion relationship books out there in the universe, and most of them are from Uranus. After reading this book, you will be able to spot them in a heartbeat. It won't take you long to see why this book is different. You will find that it not only makes a lot of sense but also is very helpful for most any and all relationships.

We Are All From Uranus

CHAPTER ONE

I Love You. You're Perfect. Now Change!

LET'S FAST-FORWARD TO THE first visit to a marriage counselor of our miserable married couple, Paul and Barbara. Remember that Paul and Barbara are feeling depressed and utterly defeated about their relationship. The setting: a room decorated in calming blues, purples, and grays. Paul and Barbara sit at opposite ends of a lush deep-violet couch, replete with fluffy pillows intended to provide comfort but that just might have also served as weapons in other couples' therapy sessions. The counselor sits across from them in his own chair and asks why they've decided to seek marriage counseling. An eerie dead silence slowly consumes the room as the tension emanating in waves from the two opponents slowly builds to a crescendo. The tension in the angry atmosphere is thick enough to cut with a knife. Then, all of a sudden, *boom!* Both immediately unleash a verbal laser attack on each other, showing no mercy.

Paul is glaring daggers at Barbara. He points an accusing finger at her.

Paul: You shouldn't talk to me the way you do. I am your husband.

Barbara leans toward him, reacting to his aggressive posture with her own.

Barbara: I wouldn't have to if you would just listen to me more often. You never pay any attention to me! What about my feelings? You could show at least a little interest in how I feel!

Paul: (*raising his eyebrows and looking shocked and angry*) Me? You're the one who is so damn self-centered. You *should* have dinner ready and keep the house cleaner. Instead, you're always on the phone with one of your ditzy girlfriends. Hell, you pay more attention to them than you do your own husband.

Barbara grits her teeth and hisses back.

Barbara: It wouldn't be that way if you treated me better. You *should*, you know—and you would if you really loved me!

Thankfully our intermediary steps in before the situation turns into a bloodbath. He gestures as if pushing Paul and Barbara apart.

Therapist: Stop! Whoa! Wait a minute. What's your goal here? Are you trying to wreck this marriage? Are you trying for an anger-resentment record? The purpose here isn't to get into a contest over who is the worst partner. So take a step back and decide whether you really want to work on saving your relationship, because this kind of insult-slinging isn't going to accomplish that.

Barbara slumps back against the couch, looking worn and defeated. She takes a deep anguished breath before responding.

Barbara: No. I want to make this marriage work, and I want to be happy. (*She glances resentfully over at Paul.*) He *should* know that and at least make an effort to change.

Paul, charged up again, angrily gestures at her.

Paul: Do you hear this?! How can it work? She is constantly a nag. I work my ass off to provide a comfortable life for our family. She *should* count her lucky stars and show some appreciation. But does she? No! She's spoiled. All she thinks about are her own needs. She *should* take a good look in the mirror and realize that she's the one who needs to change and grow up.

And here we arrive at the crux of their problem, as both shout the same two phrases at each other... simultaneously.

Barbara: *I* should change?! *You* should change!

Paul: *I* should change?! *You* should change!

Gesturing for the couple to move away from each other once again, the therapist breaks in.

Therapist: All right, calm down and put your guns away. I hear what both of you are saying, and I have a pretty good idea what's influencing and fueling the fire, the problems in your relationship. This might sound strange, but just hear me out. I think you two are from... Uranus.

Paul and Barbara, surprised and more than a little wary, both look at the therapist as if he's just grown horns and a tail. The therapist grins and holds up his hands and nods, acknowledging their reactions while reminding them to let him explain before they decide to sprint out of his office.

Men aren't from Mars and women aren't from Venus. When they argue like this, they're all from Uranus. It's apparent that you two could *should* each other to death. I think we may have to perform a "should-ectomy." (*The therapist pauses, looking pointedly at first Paul and then Barbara, and observes the puzzled look on both of their faces.*)

Look, if I'm going to help you solve your problems and help you feel good about your relationship, then let's consider learning to communicate in a healthier way. Let's stop the *should*-ing on each other. *Shoulds* sound like bullets!

When you use them, you sound like parents talking to a child, scolding each other and shaking your finger. Then each of you takes offense and upsets yourself, resulting in your defensive and angry reactions. And if you keep doing the same thing, you'll keep getting the same dismal results. Agreed?

Barbara nods. Her desperate yearning to do something—anything—to try to fix this relationship is evident in her expression. She looks cautiously over at Paul and then back to the therapist.

Barbara: I understand. Clearly, if we keep doing the same thing we're doing now, nothing will change. And we both know we could use some changes. That's why we are here.

The therapist nods and sits back, folding his hands in his lap.

Therapist: Good. Then let's get started making some healthy changes that will help you work out solutions to difficult problems. Let's work on your rigidity; that's what shoulds are. They are the rigid, chiseled-in-stone rules you learned directly from your education on Uranus. Let's help you become more flexible. Let's assume that helping you process and think about things in a more flexible way will help you work things out more simply and provide you with valuable communication tools, which will in turn help you improve your cooperative behavior. Is that worth a try? Is it a good starting point?

Paul and Barbara look at each other, then back to the therapist and nod.

Paul and Barbara: "Agreed."

Process Versus Content

Paul's and Barbara's visit was a fairly typical first visit. Frequently couples like them have been to one or more therapists and have made extraordinary efforts to be well read on the topic of relationships. They have put heroic effort and energy into attempts to solve problems within their relationship.

But one thing is readily apparent. It is not only the content or the specific problems, issues, or events that they are dealing with that is tripping them up. *It is the way they process these problems and events.* It is how they think. Their thought-processing about relationships has gone haywire. They have been infected with the unhealthy ways of thinking and relating from Uranus. *Process* simply means how you are assessing problems and producing solutions. How you process is a result of the rules of thinking and problem solving that you have learned...or not.

Everyone has a set of rules for thinking about their environment and their relationships. These rules are used for thinking about partners, kids, neighbors, coworkers, bosses, family members, or strangers. They may not be aware of their own rules, but the rules are there. These rules form the framework for the way they think about things, about everyday interactions, and especially about the way problems are dealt with in relationships. If Paul and Barbara have ineffective rules, then it makes sense that they will have difficulty getting reasonable results when they use these rules.

Think of it this way: *rational* means reasonable, logical, helpful, and healthy; *irrational* means unreasonable, illogical, unhelpful, and unhealthy. Even though all of us are typically somewhere in between these extremes at different times, if we strive to think reasonably we increase our chances for relationship success. Thinking with flawed logic gives us flawed results. As a useful model, think of the brain as working somewhat like a computer. No, of course our brains aren't computers, but using this simple analogy can help us to understand something much more complex, such as the brain. What do you think will happen if the computer has faulty software? Thinking illogically is like having faulty software in a computer. What will happen if you unthinkingly feed it a bunch of garbled nonsense? The computer will process things in a flawed manner and produce flawed results. And worse yet, faulty processing will struggle to make sense out of most any problem and will likely fail to produce sensible solutions.

> *As we look back in on our couple, they seem to be following the therapist's logic. The fighting and aggressive tension have decreased, and while they are still on opposite sides of the couch, they have stopped pointing fingers and are no longer glaring at each other. Both have been listening intently.*
>
> **Paul and Barbara:** So if our rules are unreasonable, then it is going to be hard to get positive results, the results we want.
>
> **Therapist:** Yes. You are going to learn how you can identify and change your unhealthy and unreasonable rules from Uranus. You can then exchange them, if you so desire, for healthy and reasonable rules. If you choose to institute these healthier rules, right away you will begin to see an improvement in your results. You will feel more in control of your life and your relationships. You will feel happier more often, and you will almost certainly learn to feel better about yourself and your relationships.
>
> Of course, there is no guarantee that you will never have problems. Problems are an inevitable part of living your life. But if you practice and apply these skills, you will handle your problems in a much more reasonable and practical way, which usually gets better results. You will minimize problems and maximize enjoyment. You will hold the recipe for improving your relationship right in your very own hands.

Paul's Background
Let's get to know Paul a little better. So far we've seen most of his and Barbara's relationship through her viewpoint, painting

him in a less-than-flattering light. But Paul, like Barbara and the majority of humans, is just that, a fallible human who makes mistakes. This in no way makes him a bad person, just imperfect, like the rest of us who have grown up on Uranus. So let's get to know him a little better and see the influences on why he acts the way he does today. Paul grew up always trying to please everyone, yet it seemed he got more criticism than praise. Even though he did well in school and rarely got into trouble, it wasn't good enough. He felt that his achievements went unnoticed but that every little mistake was dragged into the spotlight and carefully written down in an invisible permanent record, to be pulled out and referred to at his parents' whim. He believed he had to be perfect in order to win love and approval from his parents. Every mistake felt like a physical blow to his chest, because his parents never failed to bring out that permanent record, which grew longer and longer with each incident. They were severely critical and rigid in their beliefs, always telling him how he should be and what he should and shouldn't do. It wasn't surprising, then, that with his having been raised in such a strict and rigid environment, he learned to think with very rigid *shoulds* from Uranus.

He learned he had to be perfect to get approval and feel worthwhile. He learned to be very demanding and hard on himself and others. He tended to become easily frustrated, angry, and critical of himself and others, for even the slightest imperfection. He had learned from his parents how relationships and the world should be. And because he wanted to be the perfect husband, just as he had yearned to be the perfect son, he felt wounded when criticized.

When Paul met Barbara, he felt as though he'd been struck by lightning. She was ideal. She was lovable, warm, and pretty, and best of all, she was smitten with him. She made him feel perfect. He immediately fell in love. Paul knew she was "the one," that she was the other half he was looking for in a wife. They had a whirlwind courtship. Paul knew when their explosive kisses made him see stars that Barbara was his soul mate and was fated to be his perfect wife, as he would be her perfect husband.

Barbara's Background
Now that we've had a look at what makes Paul tick, let's see how Barbara was raised. The differences and similarities could be the key to understanding what is aggravating the conflict between them, and perhaps point to a resolution for how they can resolve it. Barbara grew up in a wonderful, caring family. She might as well have been named Barbara Cleaver. There were shoulds in her family, but they were what people might term the helpful kind. Nevertheless, Barbara did have lots of shoulds; she should make better grades, she should be more helpful, she shouldn't argue so much, she should be more like her sister, she should make her bed, she should be on time, she should, she should, she should.... These are benign-sounding shoulds. Her parents were simply trying to give her a solid value system for getting ahead in the world.

It didn't matter that her parents were not always necessarily the ones that were doing the *should*-ing as she grew up. Needless to say, she learned to should herself quite well, becoming self-sufficient and no longer requiring another person to should for her. She had taken the well-intentioned shoulds and made them into rigid demands for herself. Her parents wanted good grades; therefore, she believed she should get straight A's. They wanted her to have good manners, so she believed she should have perfect manners. Her parents were happy with her successes, so she believed she should always be successful.

It seemed, at least to her, that she must always make her parents happy. When her parents were happy, they praised her, and she liked that. It felt good, each received praise accompanied by a sharp seductive high, a feeling that grew more addicting with each experience. So Barbara always did what she should and was the perfect child. In turn, in this should-world Barbara created, she knew that one day she would, or perhaps should, meet the perfect man, her soul mate, who would always love her no matter what. She would be the perfect wife. Unfortunately, along the way she had inadvertently become riddled with shoulds. Barbara had become a should junkie. And make no mistake about it, shoulds come straight from Uranus.

Then she met Paul, and after a brief courtship, she knew that he was right for her. They laughed and had fun. He was witty, bright, charming, and handsome. He was even polite. Paul's ratings in the "possible husband material" category were off the chart. He never criticized her or told her how she should be. He accepted her, praised her, and lusted after her. She felt good about him, herself, and their relationship. Infatuation ensued, and *bingo!* She was certain Paul would be the perfect husband.

What Happened?
They got married. The honeymoon was magical. They bought the perfect house with the perfect white picket fence, and even got a puppy, practicing for the future 2.25 children that would complete their perfect family. They were two people in love! What could possibly go wrong? Well, unfortunately they both had taken the course How to Have Relationships on Uranus 101. All of their knowledge came straight from Uranus. You might have noticed when talking about relationships with friends and others, you sometimes hear comments that "everyone brings along their own...let's just say...stuff with them to the relationship." At this point in the book, we don't have to tell you where that stuff comes from. You've got it, straight from Uranus. But stuff be damned, they had overlooked another perhaps even more important problem...they never learned healthy relationship

skills. Barbara and Paul have no way of understanding or dealing with their stuff, even if they want to.

They thought, like most do, that love is as easy as falling off a rock. They also didn't know each other very well. Their fast-and-furious romance didn't leave much extra time for them to discover the not-as-lovable parts of each other and to figure out how to even start dealing with those differences. They hadn't paid attention to the warning signs, or they had blithely assumed that the other would change or be changed. They assumed they knew how to have a relationship. They really hadn't given much thought about their relationship rules from Uranus, and those beliefs about relationships are now haunting them. They had never learned to disagree. They had never learned to agree to disagree. Unbeknown to both, they were relating from Uranus.

Barbara, like many people, was afraid to speak up when things weren't going her way. She didn't like being ignored when she wanted to talk, and she didn't like it when Paul left in the morning without a good-bye kiss. Then, when the end of the day came, she felt hurt again when he didn't ask about her day. Little disappointments like these popped up around the clock, turning each new day into series of small, needling complaints, which, as we'll see, silently simmer and build up exponentially over time. Eventually, she felt taken for granted and began to conclude that he was more interested in himself than her. But she was afraid to speak up. She believed, as most people do, that complaining violates the rules of being in love. "He should know what I want and how I feel. I shouldn't have to tell him. People truly in love know what the other person needs."

As Barbara grew to know Paul better, she began to realize that he is a very different person than the one she imagined him to be when they were dating. She now feared that if she complained, he would get angry with her. He might pout like her father did and withdraw his love, ending with her feeling crushed and hurt. She believes she should be a good wife and not nag him. So she remained silent, trying to pretend the problems didn't exist... until that fateful day when "she'd had it up to here." She had been saving her complaints for months, letting them build and multiply. Eventually, the dam broke and the shoulds came spewing out. On this epic day one might call the beginning of the Shoulds War, the shoulds hit the ... fan. Might this be an all-too-common occurrence in your life?

The Punishment Contest
While Barbara was steadily amassing and cataloguing her secret list of complaints, Paul hadn't exactly been obliviously hanging out in left field. He noticed changes in Barbara as well. He too was assembling a list of disappointments from small to large in their relationship. He began to notice that Barbara was paying less and less attention to him in general and specifically paying less attention to all of the little—one might say insignificant—things she used to do for him. She didn't meet him at the door with a smile and a quick peck on the cheek anymore, or make sure that first cup of coffee was hot and ready for him when he stumbled out of bed in the morning. It was the smaller details like those and many other small things that caught his attention as one by one they disappeared, and he realized how important those small signs of affection had been to him.

He decided, however, that he was not going to make a big deal out of these little annoyances. Even so, they grew and grew—remarkably similar to what happened for Barbara—and kept on growing. As time went on and their relationship became increasingly strained, ignoring the annoying irritations became harder and harder to do. Paul figured she was just being moody, or maybe she was trying to piss him off. Whatever it was, he began to feel resentful toward her because of how she was treating him. He certainly couldn't see what the hell he had done to deserve it. He responded in a way that seems to come natural to most humans: punishing others for their errors. He began to show her less attention in the hopes of teaching her a lesson, giving her a taste of her own medicine. He was silently responding—this is where the telepathy that all humans are apparently born with but just can't seem to learn how to use comes in handy—that she was starting to get on his last nerve, and he wasn't going to just let it slide anymore. Great idea! Just what all struggling relationships need: a punishment contest! And the longer it continues, the longer Paul's list of shoulds and shouldn'ts grows, just as the penalties steadily increase for each new infraction.

Eventually Barbara removed her gloves, giving as good as she got. It was obvious that the honeymoon was over. They were now in an all-out war, and both were determined to win by punishing the other until someone cried uncle. Paul was going to ignore Barbara until she changed, and she was going to complain until he saw the error of his ways.

This is a classic technique used by small children. If you'll think back for a moment to those fights and tantrums you had as a child with siblings or friends, you may remember that this tactic didn't achieve very good results. Someone usually ended up sobbing, possibly because one person hit or pulled the hair of the other person, and parents were called in to mediate. It sounds a little bit like divorce, doesn't it? When you were a child, nobody ended up winning whatever it was they were fighting over in the first place, and everyone went home unhappy with their tail between their legs and with resentment, anger, and sadness over the situation jumbled up inside them, creating a nice little tornado of unhappiness. Of course, the kids got over it right away, but the parents often simmered, grumbling on and on about how their kids were unfairly treated and misunderstood. It appears that we haven't changed much despite growing older and supposedly wiser. Unfortunately, tattling to our parents about the unfair world doesn't really work anymore—but then, it never really did. Yet we are still drawn to bringing them into the fight as weapons, digging up memories of those earlier fights from the back of our minds—as it's hopefully been a while since we've acted this immaturely—and defaulting to the only thing we've been taught to do in this situation. Now as an adult, instead of running to Mom and Dad, we extrapolate and contort what we have learned about relations...

"You're just like my mother!"
"You're just like my father!"

$$\text{Tension} \Rightarrow \text{distance} \Rightarrow \text{arguing}$$

$$\text{Complaining} \Rightarrow \text{make-up sex} \Rightarrow \text{threats}$$

$$\text{Demands} \Rightarrow \text{tension} \Rightarrow \text{more make-up sex}$$

And the cycle continues, as if we have invented eternal recurrence. When the only higher authority available is a judge in a divorce case, a warring couple is left with just themselves as mediators.

Without knowledge of other options for resolving the conflict, Paul and Barbara continued unraveling their relationship. The periods of bad times were getting longer than the good times. The distance between the two was increasing, day by day. It finally dawned on them that there is seldom a winner in a punishment contest. At this realization, both of them became alarmed and more than a little embarrassed by their behavior, and, more than that, they felt desperation and anguish over how unhealthy and miserable their relationship had become. Remembering how wonderful it had been and seeing how much it had deteriorated, how much they had been slowly ripping it to shreds, was a devastating shock. Paul and Barbara could finally see that their relationship, which had once formed a large patchwork quilt compiling their experiences and everything that made up their lives together, and stitched together to encompass the couple, had been reduced to a pile of shreds that used to be squares. This finally jolted them into action, and they decided to seek help in the hopes that the tattered remains of their relationship could somehow be stitched back together.

Now, let's go back to our unhappy couple searching for a ray of hope inside the dismal storm looming over their relationship.

Therapist: If you two want to make some healthy changes, I'm willing to work with you. That is, if you both agree to make an effort toward learning new, healthy skills and are willing to focus individually on yourself. In other words, it is your individual responsibility to practice and use these skills. If you want to use your rules from Uranus and continue to complain about the content—that is, about what he or she does that they *should*n't do—you won't require me. You can skip to hiring lawyers to convince a judge to rule in your favor. Or I can teach you how to process your relationship problems in a healthier way.

The therapist spread his hands out to the side, looking questioningly at the both of them.

So what's it going to be? Are you willing to learn some new tools? Would you like to learn healthy rules that are incompatible with the unhealthy rules from Uranus that you have been using? Would you like to develop effective conflict-resolution skills? Do you want to have better methods of communicating with each other than the rating, blaming, rigidity, and lack of self-responsibility that you currently use from Uranus?

With these new skills, you will create fewer problems for yourself and will solve conflicts in your relationship much more easily. Understand that you have options. I can give you the tools to work on trying to mend this rift between the two of you and hopefully create stronger bonds through the use of these tools than the ones you initially formed that snapped under pressure. So there is hope, if you are willing to commit yourselves to doing the work—and it will be hard work—to use the tools that I give you and to open yourselves up to changing those unhealthy beliefs about communication and relationships you learned on Uranus.

Barbara sniffled softly and let out a sigh, brushing a sleeve under one eye where a tear had slipped past her guard. Paul cleared his throat next to her, his eyes looking a little red and watery as well, and glanced over at Barbara. She lifted her head to look back over at him, her gaze then moving to his hand extended in invitation to her. She looked back up at him, giving him a watery-eyed smile, the first smile he could recall being directed at him in months, and then she placed her hand in his. He gave her hand a small squeeze, nodded, and then they both turned to face the therapist.

When both nodded their agreement, they were given the following rules, the basic assumptions of healthy earthly relationships:

Generally Healthy Rules for Relating
1 **We are all flawed.** None of us is perfect. Remind yourself that you are not a bad person even if you behave badly from time to time. Remind yourself that the other person is also flawed and will behave poorly from time to time. Rate the behavior and not the person. Address the behavior you don't like, and avoid labeling or rating the person. Avoid rating others and avoid rating yourself; address and rate the behaviors instead. In other words, we are all fallible human beings. We all make mistakes. We are all different. And it

is generally healthier to learn from our mistakes than to beat ourselves up over them. Now we have a level playing field for relating, making it possible for you to talk to each other as equals, as two flawed and fallible human beings. Remember, we have admitted to imperfection, which puts us in the same class. There is nothing to rate, since we are equalized by our flaws.

2 **Flexibility typically gets better results than rigidity.** It is healthier for you and for your relationships if you try to think in terms of what you prefer, want, and desire as opposed to what you rigidly demand—that is, what you *must* have, *should* have, *have to* have, absolutely need, or that someone owes you. Give your opinion, but recognize that it is not a universal opinion that everyone agrees with. If everyone did agree, you wouldn't *have to* mention it, for the other person would already be doing what you want. Avoid arguing right and wrong! Discuss your opinions instead.

3 **Thoughts cause or influence feelings.** Only I can upset myself. Only I can make myself happy and unhappy. I am responsible for my own happiness. It is not what the other person has done but what I tell myself about what they have done. It is not the event that causes me to feel a certain way but rather my evaluation of the event that influences my feelings. It is my thoughts and beliefs. I upset myself by what I believe about what they did, by what I'm telling myself, my self-talk. I may not like it. I might find it annoying. But I do not *have to* upset myself about it.

So you can stop blaming and start living. Take responsibility for your thoughts, feelings, and behaviors.

Go back and review the basics assumptions again. They are very, very important.

Now you are going to learn how to use these techniques to feel good about relationships and keep your wits about you. In spite of Paul and Barbara's background, upbringing, and years of practicing unhealthy rules from Uranus, they can overcome the influence of their past. They can be more successful in their relationship fairly quickly, without years of therapy. They are going to learn how to take responsibility, stop blaming, and start living. No more "I love you! You're perfect.... Now change!"

CHAPTER TWO

There's No Self-Acceptance on Uranus

(with Bonus: One-Kick Therapy)

IF YOU ARE GOING to have intimate relationships, then it is important that you begin by learning healthy self-acceptance. If you are like a lot of others, you probably have read or heard about a ton of self-help books, most of which emphasize liking yourself and developing good self-esteem. In order to work on our relationships with others, it's important that we understand our relationship with ourselves and learn how to work on fixing us and improving our own relationship skills before we look at jumping into relationships with others. So let's start at square one. Let's work to get rid of your self-loathing or your tendency to blame others for your own shortcomings. The basis for your being able to even consider generally liking yourself starts with self-acceptance. Let's create a level playing field.

Accept that you and others are human, flawed and fallible ones at that. Try to forget about when you were little and were the center of the universe. Earth is not the center of the universe. Uranus is not the center of the universe, and neither are you. And in case you were wondering, people on Uranus forget to make that adjustment as they age and become adults. On Uranus it's not uncommon to think that the world exists "for me and me only." If you have not yet made that adjustment, it's time now to do so.

Now we've leveled the playing field, balancing it so it is not solely tilted in just your direction.

Let's go back to the healthy basic assumptions. We all have flaws. Unlike on Uranus, we are not perfect. Sure, we might know someone who thinks they are perfect: your mother in-law, your boss, and so on. We know they aren't, even if they don't. We can safely say that perfection is pretty much impossible. They are imperfect human beings, flawed and fallible, like the rest of us humans. Yes, even the most experienced experts and successful people have flaws. It just doesn't make sense to say that someone is perfectly good or even perfectly bad. For example, to say that someone is completely bad because they have one flaw—or two or three—is unhealthy and even absurd, but you still hear it frequently on Uranus. The idea of being perfect is an example of polarized black-and-white thinking. It would be very hard to find a perfectly bad person, or a perfectly good one for that matter. And here's the good news: It's okay not to be perfect. It's okay not to like some parts of you. You might not like some of the things you do or have done. You might not like something about yourself: your manners, habits, size, shape, weight, age, hair, nose, hips, or lips... or whatever.

It is okay and quite reasonable to not like certain aspects of your own self or the aspects of others. Not liking something can motivate you to work toward changing or accepting it. That might be why you are reading this book. And by doing so, you are demonstrating that you are willing to work on decreasing your unhealthy habitual patterns of thinking and behaving. You can generally like yourself and accept that you have flaws. Then, if you prefer, you can work on changing those flaws. Accepting yourself doesn't *have to* stop you from working to decrease flaws. Remember, having flaws doesn't make you a bad person. It doesn't mean you are somehow inferior or unworthy of the rest of the human race. Having flaws makes you a human. Welcome to the club. Accept yourself with the good and the bad. Then you can work on improving the qualities you like and decreasing the qualities you don't like, and also consider the preferences of others.

Paul and Barbara didn't accept themselves and certainly didn't accept their partner as having flaws. They had different rules for themselves and others, became more judgmental, and as a result created a lot of stress and distress for themselves. They finally acknowledged that their partner had flaws, but they stubbornly embraced the belief that their partner *should not* and *must not* have flaws. They also couldn't admit that they each make mistakes from time to time like all humans, or recognize that both partners in relationships sometimes make mistakes. They were very critical of themselves and their partner. They *should* on themselves and on their partner...profusely. Had they recognized that they were flawed and fallible, and "that's the way it is" for us humans, it would have been much easier for them to discuss issues and compromise. It would have been easier to build a better relationship. We will deal more with their malignant Uranian *should*-ing in the next chapter and show you how this made meaningful intimate communication all but impossible in their relationship. After all, how are you going to solve problems and complaints without healthy communication?

And it's important to note that how you communicate with yourself, how you think, your self-talk, significantly influences how you communicate with your partner. "Okay. But how do I learn to accept and deal with myself as a flawed and fallible human being," you ask? Well, here's the first step: listen to your self-talk. Listen to what you say to yourself. This will take a lot of effort and practice because it is somewhat unfamiliar to most people. If you constantly put yourself down and rate yourself poorly all day, how do you expect to feel at the end of the day? Lousy, the same way most anyone would feel who belittles themselves throughout the day.

The Crooked Scorekeeper From Uranus
It is very common on Uranus, whenever people do something they think is good, whether it is a thought, a feeling, or a behavior, for them to mark their internal scorecard with a plus. Whenever they do something they think is bad, they mark it with a minus, but these negative marks are typically in bold and underlined, and sometimes a few extras are added for good measure. At the end of the day, they add up all the pluses and minuses and assess how they feel. It seems like it is almost always a negative feeling, even if there are more pluses than minuses. When asked how that could be, they typically report that a particular minus counted double, triple, or quadruple, because it was so awful. Is it just that they use bad math, perhaps? It appears that they have a very crooked scorekeeper in their head who inflates the negatives, perhaps giving negatives as much as four or five times the weight of one positive. Sometimes, even just one negative wipes out all the positives and equals *awful*. This crooked scorekeeper has been there for years, keeps us safely out of harm's way, but is incredibly efficient at magnifying misery. We can describe it as the habit of awfulizing. Awfulizing is something that most all of us have done at some point in our lives, some more than others. It can become chronically debilitating, but it usually responds well to therapy.

The first step in overcoming your crooked scorekeeper is to catch yourself mentally and verbally beating yourself up. You usually do this, at least in part, with the *shoulds*. If you make a mistake or do something you feel bad about, it is much healthier to admit it:

> I screwed up. It wasn't intentional, but I goofed. It doesn't make *me* a screw-up or a goof. It doesn't make *me* an inadequate person, a dummy, a lowly worm, or the growth between the toes of that guy I know who never changes his socks (you know, the one who can clear the room by taking off his shoes). I'm not going to label *myself* a bad person. It just proves me to be fallible. I will try to learn from my mistake and try not making it again. I will turn it into a positive by learning from it. And you can bet I'm going to do my best to keep a keen eye on my mental and physical hygiene.

On the other hand, you could try using approaches from Uranus. You can deny the mistake and argue long into the night that it was not an error. You can doggedly defend what you did. Denial and defensiveness are usually not very helpful ingredients in a relationship, however. You can try to blame the mistake on someone else, but that's not a very good way to gain popularity. Of course, a very common reaction is to flail away and try to perfect beating yourself up over it.

I shouldn't have made the mistake!

Why not? How did you get to be the exception to reality? You're not human?

I should have known better!

Really! I guess your crystal ball was malfunctioning.

I am such a stupid idiot for having made the mistake...again!

Now you've created a new intelligence test that automatically assesses willing participants round the clock. Your intelligence goes up and down hourly, depending on whether you make a mistake.

I always make mistakes!

A perfect mistake maker—we're pretty sure you've just set a world record!

I'm totally worthless, and I'll never be any good for anything.
I am an awful, terrible, total failure of a person.

No, no, and no. Again, the mistake may seem stupid, but that will never prove you to be a stupid person, even when you make certain mistakes repeatedly. And to label yourself a total failure because you repeated the same mistake is a gross overgeneralization.

When you compare, rate, and label, you are comparing yourself to perfection. You are rating yourself as an abysmally low person and justifying it with your crooked scorekeeper. By comparing and self-rating, you are putting yourself down. You are beating yourself up for not being perfect. Even if you make a mistake more than once, try not to exaggerate. Put it in perspective. You are not a total failure. If you were, that would be a world record, which would result in your actually being the best at something, negating said world record, and making you only a semi-failure. So look on the bright side: It is actually impossible for anyone, including you, to be a total failure. Try to turn your newfound insight that you have made the mistake, more than once, into a plan to improve. Then work to reduce the errors by putting the corrective plan into action. Learn from your mistakes.

Using self-rating and labeling is seldom beneficial. Look, you can most always find something in another person, a trait, that you think is better than yours... unless you hold the world record for that particular thing, and even then someone will eventually come along and beat it. So continuing to go around self-rating is essentially an unhealthy habit and a pointless waste of energy. You will often be needlessly putting yourself down, upsetting yourself, and deflating your view of yourself—or pumping yourself up to larger than life, which is also unhealthy. It's hardly worth it. Accept that we all have pluses and minuses. That doesn't make you a faulty person. It's a fact of life. Learn to get a grip on this unhealthy habit, accept your imperfect nature, and proceed in a healthier direction.

So enough with pulverizing yourself with the negativity! It's obvious that unhealthy self-talk distracts you and results in needlessly disturbing yourself. While you are worrying and debating your worth as a person, you are not concentrating on changing and improving your performance. You are inadvertently making it easier to screw up again. Break the cycle.

Oh, by the way, do you know where you learned most of this stuff? You learned it growing up as a little kid, an unaware, naive little kid from Uranus. Do you know what the really sad thing is? You still believe it. What's wrong with this picture? Have you noticed that up to this point we have been pretty much talking about "you"? Did you notice a bit of a parental tone and the accumulating weight from the "you, you, you" without respite? With most of the attention on "you," worrying about your adequacy or inadequacy can trap you in a real pickle. In other words, there is a healthier way to go about resolving this self-esteem dilemma that we created ourselves. We can simply replace the concept of self-esteem with self-acceptance. We can begin replacing and adjusting the unhealthy habit of self-esteem learned from Uranus with the healthier habit of self-acceptance that applies to all of us earthlings. That is, we can learn from our humble earthly existence to accept our plight as imperfect human beings who screw up from time to time. By noticing and changing our perspective, we can better acknowledge where the "heat" is pointed and take the self-induced heat off of ourselves. We can speak up or take a time-out when we've "had enough," or consider shifting to participating in other activities for the time being. Rather than worrying about esteem and adequacy, we can feel good about ourselves and accept our flawed and fallible nature at the same time.

Consider the pitfalls of this self-esteem strategy: While we are worrying about whether we are an adequate person, we distract ourselves from whatever it is we are trying to do. The odds then go up that we will make a mistake because we are distracted by worry. It tends to become a self-fulfilling prophecy. We worry about whether we are okay. While distracted by our worrying, we are more likely to make a mistake. Once we make a mistake, we then label ourselves as a screw-up but think we *shouldn't* be. We then continue beating ourselves up eternally.

Self-acceptance will help you recognize that you are a flawed and fallible human being who will make mistakes from time to time. Yes, you may make the same mistake more than once. Concentrate on what you are trying to accomplish, your goals. Refuse to compare and label yourself. Avoid comparing yourself to the perfect person or the imperfect person that you are trying "to be or not to be" (apologies to Shakespeare). "If you are not perfect, then you *must* be an awful person." Do you see the faulty logic? Alas, we are all flawed and fallible, so hopefully we are all changing and improving our thinking for the better.

In turn, if we do not have the healthy thinking skills necessary to accept ourselves as flawed and fallible humans, it's a good bet that we won't be able to apply the concept to our partner. A healthy relationship starts with you. For example, if you see yourself as an inadequate, lowly Uranian worm of a person, you might also believe that your partner is a superior person who gives you value. You could easily put your partner on a pedestal, only to be disappointed or enraged when they prove they are flawed and fallible. Or what if you practice with them the same thing that you practice with yourself: Uranian self-rating and labeling that leads to condemnation and damnation whenever they prove they are human? That is "disaster de jour" straight from Uranus, and not exactly a recipe for a healthy and happy relationship. On Uranus, people talk up or down to others depending on how they have rated them. They have difficulty talking across to other people, as equals, as flawed and fallible. Ditch the rating and labeling regardless if they are white, black, yellow, blue, male, or female. Accept that all of us are composites, flawed and fallible, and level the playing field.

Keep reminding yourself that it starts with you. You most likely have been trained, perhaps inadvertently, in a very Uranian way, to be your own worst enemy—as well as your partner's. You have earned a black belt in the arts of finger-wagging, criticizing, rating, and labeling yourself and others. Can you see why Paul and Barbara had so much difficulty with their flawed and fallible partner? Do you ever do the same thing? We'd be surprised if you said no. And by all means, it's okay to nod your head yes. No one is looking, and if they are, they will probably think you are cleverly nodding a self-accepting nod.

Of course this isn't all there is to it. But stop and think how it might apply to you and yours.

One-Kick Therapy

Now, just so we don't get ahead of ourselves, it's important to remember that self-deprecation from Uranus is a hard habit to break. Some people have extraordinary difficulty in breaking the habit, so it is okay to occasionally cut them a little slack. It's called one-kick therapy. Of course the optimum plan is to not kick yourself at all. But if you insist on kicking yourself, as many people do, you are allowed one kick...only one...no more. Kick yourself once, apologize to others if appropriate, and move on. Then resist and refuse any further attempts to kick yourself again. When you make a mistake, tell yourself: "There, one kick.

I did it, I kicked myself once, and now I can accept that I am a flawed and fallible human being."

You will be learning how not to pulverize yourself with punishment and guilt until you are a pathetic, sniveling heap of misery on the floor. Have some mercy on yourself. Along the way you may notice that you eventually start forgetting to kick yourself, or at least not so severely. That's okay; in fact, that's great. You might even notice you are smiling more.

Remember, you are learning how not to be your own worst enemy, and how to be a better friend to yourself. You are also learning how to avoid needlessly upsetting yourself for being a flawed and fallible human being. You are learning how not to compare your self-worth with others' worth by rating and labeling. Practice hard, and, believe it or not, you'll be in a better mood, and you will relate much more pleasantly to others...even partners. In this chapter we (yep, let's remind ourselves of that "we," since we are all on this journey called life and are learning how to best navigate it together) have learned the shortcomings of the rules from Uranus and discovered the importance of self-acceptance in creating a foundation for healthy thinking. In the next chapter, we will discover how to eliminate the dreaded *shoulds* from Uranus, something every couple *should* do.

Don't forget that Uranus is not the center of the universe!

CHAPTER THREE

The *Should*-ectomy...

Exorcising the Shoulds *From Uranus*

Eliminating Rigid Thinking

Obviously, two people from Uranus with rigid beliefs will have trouble negotiating and compromising. These are two very important skills for solving problems in relationships. Closed-minded, rigid thinking keeps people from listening and communicating in a reasonable way. Would you agree that listening is a very important component of communication skills, skills that are very important in a healthy relationship? On Uranus, people get so entrenched in defending their rigid beliefs and preparing their next proof that they are *right* in their argument that they fail to listen. "I *must* prove that I am right and you are wrong!" But it's not about right and wrong. It's about opinions. They may be important opinions to you, but alas, they are only opinions. Do you see where the black-and-white concepts of right and wrong promote rigidity? This rigidity easily leads to arguments and hinders conflict resolution. With the flexibility offered by opinions, it is much easier to listen to someone else's viewpoint and negotiate options for resolving conflicts. The dire *need to* be right is a relationship felony; it kills communication.

Guess what word is frequently at fault for this rigid thinking. That's right: *should*. *Shoulds* also have some cousins that are closely related: *must, have to, got to, ought to,* and *need to*. Then there are the overgeneralizations that often tag along with the *shoulds*—that is, *always* and *never*—that are highly characteristic of black-and-white thinking. We are going to go on record as telling you that there is rarely anything you *should* do, *must* do, *have to* do, or *need to* do. Everything is generally a choice. They might all seem like poor choices. But nevertheless, they are choices. Even though you may not *have to*, it may frequently be better or best if you do. Yes, if you want to live, you require food, water, and shelter as essentials. Everything after that is fluff. Yes, it's nice to have many of the things in life that seem to add significant quality to your life—job, family, money, health, and so on. Those and many other things can add enjoyment, quality, and happiness and reduce hassles and stress. But they are not necessities that you *must* have, and you are certainly not guaranteed them so that they *should* and *must* come your way.

On Uranus people insist on arguing that *shoulds* are necessary. They clutch them tightly all the way to their grave. It is part of their rigid thinking. As you read on, you will see that there are much more useful and productive ways to think and express yourself. It would probably be nice if you never used those rigid words, but quite likely you will from time to time. Attempt to avoid *should*-ing on yourself or others. But when it happens, remind yourself that it is generally in your best interest to choose less-rigid words. You have the power and control to decide. Some *shoulds* may seem relatively benign. However, it's good practice to work on eliminating all of them that you can, especially the ones that you use to upset yourself or direct anger at others.

Why are *shoulds* so unhealthy?

Shoulds Represent "Unarguable Laws of the Universe"
- **Law 1: You have no choice.** When you use *should* and its cousins, you are saying, and others are hearing, that you have no choice. But obviously, you do have other choices. They may be poor ones or worse ones, but they remain choices nevertheless. When you use *should*, you are stating that it is an immutable law of the universe. It is a truth that is chiseled onto a granite stone locked in some hidden, secret, hermetically sealed vault on Uranus, where all the other "truths of the world" are kept, and you are obviously the only one who has access to them. Give us a break! We don't think so!
- **Law 2: Okay, you do have a choice, but you *should* do it my way.** Translation: "If you pick any other way but mine, it labels you as a jerk and a total idiot and you *should* feel incredibly guilty." The *should* implies that there is a right way and wrong way to do something, and occasionally that may be the case. But it also implies that good people will pick my way—the *right* way—and that slime molds, worms, nitwits, and jerks will pick a different way. "I know the right way, and you *should* feel totally guilty and stupid if you disagree. Only an idiot would do something different!" If you want to start an argument with someone, a surefire way to do this is to call them a name, to label them. Imply that they are dumber than dirt, the village idiot, no good, or even a lumpish beef-witted clotpole, if you feel the urge to get creative. If you want to start an argument with yourself, do the same thing. If you want to feel really guilty, you can profusely *should* on yourself, and you will be almost guaranteed instant guilt! Now, is this a healthy way to treat ourselves?

Most everyone from Uranus has different *shoulds*. And guess what? They learned their *shoulds* somewhere along life's road, just like most everyone else did. *Shoulds* are learned from parents, relatives, teachers, friends, celebrities, the media, books, and so on. Line up 100 people and ask them how the world *should* be and how people *should* act. You will find an incredibly large number of different *shoulds*. Are they all correct? Hardly so—they are all opinions. The *shoulds* exist only in their minds and on Uranus. Unfortunately, although you probably innocently learned them during your golden upbringing, you continue to practice them today, unaware, even when they are unhealthy and contribute to significant conflict.

Do you know why you still use them? It's habit. An unhealthy habit from Uranus...it's that simple. You may reply, "Well, I *should* pay my rent, or I'll get thrown out." Time out! Most likely, *it would be better* if you paid your rent. That is, especially if you don't want to get thrown out. But why *must you* insist on stating it as a law of the universe? After all, it isn't. People sometimes skip rent payments for a variety of reasons. Perhaps skipping a payment isn't the best choice at that particular time, but the option of not paying exists whether you choose it or not. Just like you can choose or choose not to continue using the word *should*.

Does it sound strange to hear someone pointing out the liabilities of *shoulds*? Especially when every day of our life we have been inundated with the wonderfulness and magical wisdom of the *shoulds* and *should nots* of the universe. But *shoulds* are a habit, an unhealthy habit. Probably no one has ever pointed out to you before that *shoulds* and their cousins contribute to mental rigidity and are unhealthy. Perhaps no one ever taught you how to replace them with healthier thinking, preferential thinking. If you insist on keeping your *shoulds*, go ahead. There is no law that says you *must* or *should* give them up. Suffer or even enjoy them if you want. Nonetheless, you might want to take a long look at the disadvantages of keeping them and the advantages of replacing them with preferential thinking. Bear in mind that you only live in this world; you don't run it. You are not privy to the vault on Uranus that contains all the truths of the world. You are not the sheriff of the universe or the sheriff of Uranus. You are just passing through, as are all the rest of us humans.

Mind you, some *shoulds* are relatively benign, but it is good practice to at least work at replacing all of them that you can. Replace them with preferential thinking. Consider using phrases such as "I would prefer," "I think it is better," "I think it is best," and "It's my opinion." You will find that this sounds a lot less like nagging and is more easily accepted by your partner. What is your goal anyway? To continue to think from Uranus, to upset yourself, to argue with your partner, to be the self-professed keeper of all the truths of the universe, to show others how inferior they are and how superior you are, to have control and get things your way?

Preferential thinking is a method of communicating that enhances the flexibility of problem solving in relationships. Preferential thinking replaces *should*-ing on your partner, and of course you know by now: "You *shouldn't* do that." Thinking and speaking preferentially greatly enhances conflict-resolution skills. It allows for discussing your concerns as opinions, allowing you to inform your partner of your preferences in a reasonable and less threatening manner.

Disadvantages of Keeping Rigid Thinking
- ***Shoulds* contribute to problems because you are stating your opinions in a dogmatic, rigid way** that leaves no room for discussion, negotiation, or compromise. "It *should* be done this way because it is the only right way." It's my way or the highway!
- ***Shoulds*, like *right* and *wrong*, are trailing indicators with poor accuracy in their prediction of future outcomes** in the kind of highly dynamic, uncertain world in which we live. They do have great hindsight accuracy if we

choose to drive through life looking only in the rearview mirror. If we drove our cars like that, we would probably end up in an accident. So why would we want to drive like that through life and relationships? *Shoulds* are vacuous and empty of information.

- ***Shoulds* promote arguments because the word *should* creates a parental atmosphere**, making it easy for the recipient to perceive that the *should* user views them as having childlike inferiority. *Should* is like a parent scolding a child: "You *should* do what I say, because I know better, and only a blithering idiot wouldn't do it my way."
- ***Shoulds* deny the reality of choices** and the reality that others make choices different from your own. "That is just the way it *should* be, and there are no other choices."
- ***Shoulds* take the focus off consequences and redirect attention to the kind of person who makes that choice.** The spotlight is now on whether you think the *person* is stupid rather than whether you like their choice or opinion. "Don't be stupid. This is the way it *should* be done." *Shoulds* eliminate the possibility of differences in opinion. When you instead allow for such differences and let someone know why you think it would be better to do something a certain way, it is because you think the consequences might be better by making a particular choice. "I think it would be best to look at more options and try to choose the option that has the best chance of getting the best results."
- ***Shoulds* constrict your viewpoint on reality and your position in the world.** "It *shouldn't* be that way." Well, when you run the world, you can change it. Until then, you are not the center of the universe. Express your preferences, your likes and dislikes, but refrain from declaring as reality that all things *should* and *must* go as you decree. Recall

that you can have your preferences, but you may not always get things your way. The world does not revolve around you.
- ***Shoulds* increase the possibilities for you to upset yourself needlessly without recourse.** "The world, or my world, *shouldn't* be so awful." "That *shouldn't* have happened." The *should*-er is likely to miss the point and not see what can be done to either change things or accept them. Things happen, maybe for lots of different reasons, but the fact is that they do happen. You may not like the outcome. You may prefer that it had happened differently. Try to change things if you so desire, but upsetting yourself about outcomes, especially ones that you had no control over, hardly sounds reasonable.
- ***Shoulds* create arbitrary constraints and significant stress.** "I *should* be perfect.... I *should* get everything done on time and perfectly." But if that exceeds your ability? Sometimes we just don't finish everything we would like to get done in a single day. That's okay, all of us fallible humans experience this—yes, even the seemingly perfect ones.
- ***Shoulds* cause guilt, needless self-criticism, poor self-acceptance, and self-loathing.** "I *shouldn't* have done that. I *should* be prettier/handsomer/more efficient. Good people/efficient people/wonderful people do it right the first time. I didn't. I'm a lowly worm of a person.... I feel so guilty." What a perfect way to become your own worst enemy. When you *should* on yourself, you will likely end up feeling guilty. Likewise, when you *should* on others, you tend to start feeling anger toward them when they don't meet your rigid expectations.

Advantages of Using Preferential Thinking
By using preferential thinking, you present your opinions in a flexible way. This leaves room for discussion. This includes

phrases such as "I would rather," "I would prefer," "it would be better," and "I think it is best." You don't *have to* prove you are right. It is your opinion. Do you have reasonable information and plausible evidence for your opinions? Then preferences are likely the best the way to express them.

- **Preferential thinking allows you to recognize that you are dealing with other flawed and fallible humans**, and it leaves room for you to consider their flawed and fallible opinions. You are therefore better able to listen to their opinions on a more equal basis and perhaps even find that a compromise between those opinions is the best answer, a possibility you wouldn't have even considered before.
- **Preferential thinking and expression implies that you and others have choices**, and that you and others are responsible for those choices: "I would prefer to do it this way.... I think this is the best way.... I think this way will get the best results."
- **Preferential thinking lets you view the world and other people the way that they are.** It is called reality: "I don't like it.... I would prefer it not be that way.... I will work to change it.... But alas, it is that way." Even if there are things you don't like, you can choose not to upset yourself needlessly about them.
- **Preferential thinking allows you to be realistic about your abilities** and put your best effort forward without needlessly criticizing yourself for being a flawed and fallible human being. This allows almost instant self-acceptance.
- **Preferential thinking allows you to be your own best friend.** You no longer *have to* beat yourself up for all the things you *should* or *shouldn't* have done.

Dare to listen to yourself over a day's time. How many times do you think you use *should* or its cousins: 10 times, 100, 1,000? Are you the world record holder? Whatever the number, you probably missed quite a few of them. It is probably very unusual for you, like most people, to think about each word you use when you are thinking or talking. On Uranus it is unheard of. You will notice that it takes significant effort to screen your own thoughts as well as your speech. Don't give up. It will slowly become easier and may even become quite natural after a while. Remember that most people don't screen and edit their thoughts and speech. The way they think and speak now is the way that they have done so for a long time and has become an implicit process of habit. It will take a purposeful, explicit effort to replace these unhealthy habits of thinking and speaking with healthier ones. In other words, we can make our thinking explicit and become more in tune with how we are relating to ourselves and others.

Habits Take Work to Overcome
We learned these unhealthy thought and speech processes at an early age along with other unhealthy thinking processes, and they have taken on the force of habit. It is quite likely you learned to think in *shoulds* at an early age. The *shoulds* and other rigid thinking have become habits of old, and old habits are hard to break. By not making a conscious and concerted effort to replace these unhealthy thought processes with healthy ones, you are inadvertently continuing to practice and reinforce your unhealthy thinking. You are in effect working to keep the unhealthy processes alive. Breaking the habit might take you a while and will require effort. Not breaking the habit is worse, and the longer you wait to do it, the stronger that habit will grow. You add to and reinforce a protective steel wall around it each time you defer back to that habit, making it harder and harder

to break over time. If you keep working at learning and using healthy thinking, the odds are that you will eventually become proficient. Hmm... that concept has a nice ring to it: developing healthy habits rather than ignoring and reinforcing unhealthy habits from Uranus.

How long do you think it took Barbara and Paul to become fluent in preferential thinking? That's right. It took months and months, and they still continue to work at it. It is like learning a foreign language. The more often you practice, the more fluent you will become. We hope you are beginning to see why relationships on Uranus are so unsuccessful. On Uranus they use *should, must, have to, got to, ought to,* and *need to.* They avoid preferential statements such as "it would be better," "I would rather," and "I would prefer." Do you get the idea? Before we move on, take a look at the exercises at the end of the book in the appendices. While working on using preferential thinking, go to Exercise 3-1 in Appendix II. This will help you improve your preferential thinking skills and help you give up or at least significantly reduce your rigid thinking. Remember: practice, practice, and more practice!

Reminder

Exercise 3-1, "Decreasing *Shoulds*
and Increasing Preferential Thinking,"
in Appendix II, "Exercises,"
is highly recommended.

CHAPTER FOUR

Where Do Feelings Come From?

Mars? Venus? Uranus?

Have you ever noticed how often people talk about feelings? How others frequently ask you how you feel about something or yourself? How often are the words *feeling* and *thought* used interchangeably? When a thought is described as a feeling, someone may say, "I didn't feel like going," when they really meant, "I didn't want to go and chose not to." Or someone might ask you, "How do you feel about that?" Does that mean that they want to know how you feel emotionally? Are you happy, sad, excited, or mad? In turn, they may ask you, "What do you think about that?" Does that mean that they want to know your opinion? This chapter clarifies the differences between thoughts and feelings and talks about where feelings come from.

Feelings are important. People are frequently motivated by their feelings. If you don't feel good about doing something, the odds lessen that you will actually do it. If you do feel good about it, then you will be more motivated and more likely to do it. Feelings are vital to us humans. They are a very powerful force for helping us to steer toward what we want and steer clear of what we don't want. But here is where we can stumble into a sticky situation: We sometimes get misled by our feelings. Sometimes things that feel bad aren't necessarily bad for us. And yes, things that feel good aren't always good for us.

It is usually beneficial to stop and evaluate the choices that you have and their possible consequences, not just your feelings about them. Are the likely consequences reasonable? Are they the ones you want? Are the consequences best for you not only now but also in the long run? When people are misled by their feelings, they have a very hard time getting what they want. They are thwarted by their moods and emotions, such as anger, anxiety, guilt, and sadness. This frequently leads to poor choices that result in much suffering. Feelings may even lead a person to avoid things that are good for them and gravitate toward things that aren't good for them. Having an understanding of where feelings come from, and how we developed so many myths and misconceptions about them, will help you make better decisions and choices in your life. Knowing where feelings come from is also especially helpful when it comes to choosing and implementing new healthy skills for the benefit of your relationships. So where do feelings come from?

Where Do Feelings Really Come From?

First of all, quit pointing to your heart, stomach, or some planet. That is not where feelings come from. You can skip over this explanation if you like, but you may find it gives you a clearer picture of all this love-and-feelings stuff. This is somewhat of an oversimplification, but humans and other primates have two main parts of the brain that are mostly responsible for feelings and behavior: the limbic system and the cerebral cortex.

The limbic system is the primary seat of emotions; it's at the heart (pun intended) of the seemingly mysterious place our feelings stem from. The limbic system is our original primal brain and shares many common features with the brains of other mammals and primates. In addition to this part of our brain, we have the cerebral cortex, which is responsible for deliberate thought. The cerebral cortex is generally larger and more developed in humans. This "bigger and better" brain, along with human language, sets us apart from other primates by providing an ability to evaluate not only our surroundings but ourselves as well.

The cerebral cortex is responsible for higher-level *executive* thinking, meaning that it is capable of making complex decisions and can be used for solving complex problems. It also affords us the luxury of highly developed language and communication skills. We can actually think about thinking. We can think about *how* we think—remember that sneaky self-talk. We can even change the way we think, with some effort. We can reprogram and replace old, unhealthy mental software with newer, more up-to-date, healthier mental software. The cerebral cortex also has the incredible ability to stop, reflect, and override emotions, by deliberately thinking things through and following our higher-level thought processes rather than automatically following our emotional lower-level limbic system. In other words, we have a choice. It is up to us to think things through in a reasonable manner and make the best choices for how we think and behave.

The limbic system is involved in many emotions, including anger, fear, guilt, disgust, love, and happiness, and gives us a sense of feeling comfortable and secure with what is familiar. The limbic system is also probably the culprit for other feelings, such as feeling bonded to others—like emotional glue. Do you remember all the happy thoughts and how great it feels when you are in love and bonding to someone? Then you probably also remember breaking up... and all the accompanying negative thoughts and how bad it felt when that bond was broken. Bonding helps to keep couples together. Have you ever had a broken heart? What people are referring to as their heart is actually the feelings generated by their limbic system.

Recall that things that feel good aren't always good for you and things that feel bad aren't always bad for you. Sometimes people stay in very unhealthy and unpleasant relationships to avoid the pain of breaking the bond. You could choose to go with your limbic system and stay in the relationship without thinking through your choices and evaluating the possible consequences, thus avoiding the pain of breaking the bond. Or you have the choice of choosing to leave regardless of the pain because you think it is in your best interest to do so.

It is entirely in your power to pick one method or another, but it will still require a lot of effort. Your old irrational software that is currently occupying your cerebral cortex is unable to make sense of the feelings generated by your limbic system. Therefore, it is pretty common for people to use their cerebral cortex to justify and rationalize the frequently irrational choices that are behind their thoughts and behaviors. It also results in their coming up with some pretty silly explanations for those choices. Obviously, this wreaks havoc on relationships. Do you see how feelings can sometimes be misleading? It is important to listen to what you are thinking, or what you are telling yourself—your self-talk.

You have already learned that the cerebral cortex is responsible for executive functions such as evaluating your choices for your thoughts and your behaviors. The cerebral cortex is also responsible for identifying and monitoring your self-talk. By listening to your self-talk, you can identify whether you are telling yourself something that is unhealthy and irrational or whether you are instead telling yourself something healthy and rational. The cerebral cortex is clearly very important when it comes to relationships. It is the same part of your brain that helps you evaluate the possible outcomes for your choices and decide if the choices are in your best interest. Your cerebral cortex is also responsible for helping you use the things you are learning in this book to improve your relationship skills. When you are learning and using the knowledge from this book, you are reprogramming your cerebral cortex. You are replacing unhealthy software with healthy software.

Use your cerebral cortex to evaluate your limbic system rather than the other way around. You can passively choose to let your limbic system be in charge of your relationships, or you can actively choose to reprogram and use your cerebral cortex to take charge of your relationships. You can learn to think and actively plan ahead rather than reactively after the fact. If you want the best results, you can choose to use your brain to preferentially navigate through life and relationships and to help you deal more reasonably with your "heart." That is, consider prioritizing your deliberate-thinking cerebral cortex over blindly following your automatic limbic system.

In the Beginning
On Uranus, misconceptions about the origin of feelings are planted early on in childhood development and prior to adolescence, when there is very concrete, black-and-white thinking. During that time there is an infusion of unhealthy concepts, resulting in imprinting irrational and faulty software onto the young, computer-like brain. On Uranus, kids are not only taught to think in terms of *should, must, have to, got to, need to*, and so on. They are also taught that others cause their feelings.

These concepts are reinforced by their parents, and by most of society. Can you believe it? Can you believe that anyone would teach such nonsense, that other people cause your feelings and that you cause their feelings? That is pretty incredible; we apparently have been born with the ability to control others' minds. No *need* for that expensive love potion. We can just make the other person love us; we can bend them to our incredible will. When you were a child, did you ever hear statements like these? "Don't make your father angry." "You hurt your sister's feelings." "You made me angry." Well, guess what? We carry these concepts from Uranus into adulthood, where they'll stay unless we challenge and replace them. On Uranus, they forgot to mention to us that mind control apparently comes without a user's manual and thus no one can figure out exactly how controlling others' feelings works. Of course that doesn't seem to stop us from blaming this mythical control for all sorts of feelings. Well, it's time to put on your big-girl panties or big-boy knickers and challenge that nonsense from Uranus.

You have probably seen the following interaction: a well-intentioned parent innocently teaching a toddler that others are responsible for their feelings. A toddler is wandering around and falls, without serious injury. The toddler starts whimpering, looking toward the parent, and begins running to them. The concerned parent immediately reaches for the toddler and says, "Here, sweetie, let me make it feel better." Even though there are no malicious intentions, the message is that others can make you feel a certain way and that they are responsible for how you feel.

Now, if you are a parent, have ever baby-sat, or have ever come in some contact with children, you may have noticed another, generally more effective parental reaction in this scenario. So imagine once again that this toddler falls while playing on the playground, as toddlers tend to do from time to time. The toddler shoots the same pitiful, tearful gaze straight toward the parent. However, this time, instead of making a big fuss over what appears to be a small scratch, the parent states, while calmly pointing to the offending limb, "You're all right. See? It's just a small scratch. It's nothing too bad." Rather than going into hysterics, the child is able to look and evaluate, and may then run off to play again. This allows the child to actually examine their own feelings over the incident and its outcome.

You might have noticed that when children get into scrapes that their reaction often stems from the parent's reaction. If the parent gets upset, so does the child. But if the parent stays calm and doesn't call undue attention to the wound, the child has an opportunity to stay calmer and assess how the injury feels to them, usually deciding it's not bad enough to keep them from jumping back to their feet and continuing with their plans to get into mischief and create mayhem for all those in the vicinity. While this method is by no means foolproof, it helps to spark the child's use of the deliberately thinking cerebral cortex rather than automatically letting the limbic system take over.

The first example, however, is a fairly common occurrence, and just one of the many ways that parents and society begin to reinforce the myth that others are responsible for our feelings. Even when the parents have the best of intentions in offering to help the child "feel better," the child may start to believe that the parent can make them feel good whenever they hurt. It might not be long before they start to blame the parent for their hurts, especially when the parent doesn't fix them. Sure, the parent is responsible for the child's welfare. Wounds, cuts, scratches, and abrasions can be taken care of with a tincture of TLC and concern *and without taking responsibility for the pain*. But unfortunately, parental habit of taking responsibility for the child's feelings frequently extends into the child's adulthood. Extended responsibility for feelings can lead to very complicated and dysfunctional relationships between parents and their grown children—and yes, in intimate relations. Typically, individual responsibility for feelings is never clarified. And the parent fails to differentiate between taking responsibility for the child's well-being, comfort, and safety versus taking responsibility for the child's feelings.

You cannot control the feelings of your child. In other words, you can't upset your child or make them happy, even though you might influence their feelings. You can do things for them, but they may or may not perceive it in the way you prefer. While you might be able to cause or relieve physical pain and you might influence emotional pain, it is important for children to learn the difference, including their increasing individual responsibility for their own feelings when interacting with others. Of course, we can point out that our behavior influences the environment and that consideration of others' feelings makes sense. You might attend to someone who is in emotional pain. You might try to comfort them. But it is only what they tell themselves about your intervention that affects their feelings. You could tell them, "I'm so sorry you feel so bad," and put your arm around them. And they could tell themselves, "He doesn't understand. No one understands," and become even more upset. Of course, they could also tell themselves, "How nice of her to try to help. I really appreciate it," and subsequently feel better. Doing something for someone is one thing, and it is frequently admirable. Being concerned about how the person feels is also very important. But taking responsibility for their feelings exceeds the boundaries of human ability. What is the relationship between thoughts and feelings? Typically, a large influence on how a person feels emotionally is their self-talk.

Later On
You are innocently trotting down the path of life when out of the blue, you are ambushed by an insult. Maybe you are the unfortunate new kid at school or new adult at work, which relegates you to the unenviable position of lackey and makes it liable that you'll receive a certain amount of hazing or bullying before being accepted. Maybe it's even worse than that and you have the boss from hell. Regardless, this particular day begins on a high note;

you get to where you're going on time, you're minding your own business, and the day seems to be proceeding smoothly. You are at lunch, blissfully unaware of danger approaching, eating your chicken salad sandwich, when someone comes up to you and loudly proclaims that you are the dumbest, stupidest, ugliest, and lousiest, most incompetent, sorry excuse for a person they have ever seen, met, or heard about. Your eyes open as wide as saucers and your hands stop halfway to bringing said sandwich to your now slack jaw; you are in total shock.

What the hell just happened? Of course, you don't like "feeling like" you were insulted (you prefer not to be spoken to that way), but you still have options for how to react to it. You could tell yourself, "Oh no, she *shouldn't* talk to me like that. How dare she upset me like this! She's supposed to like me and respect me—treat me with dignity, for crying out loud! This is a disaster that someone thinks I am a terrible person. My day is now officially ruined." You could then continue mumbling to yourself in disbelief while your sandwich slowly slides from your shaking hands and plops to the floor. "Everyone is supposed to like me. I thought they did. I'm the witty friend who provides laughter and joy, as well as the occasional shoulder to cry on. I can't handle being treated this way." And then you could run crying to the nearest bathroom...as if you are auditioning for the role of drama queen!

On the other hand, you could say to the person, "Tell me how you really feel about me,' or "What you think about me is none of my business," and laugh it off. Or you could say to yourself, "Wow, they really seem upset." You might reply with something like "You sound upset about something. Do you want to talk about it?" In saying that, you have just generated concern rather than anger. You didn't make it personal and didn't upset yourself.

Let's turn our attention to identical twins Susie and Sally. Both are blond-haired, blue-eyed cheerleaders for their high school football team and enjoy the much-sought-after status of being part of the popular crowd in their school's rigid and competitive student hierarchy. Appearances, however, can be deceiving. Place both girls in a confrontation where someone tells both that they are ugly, hated, and worth less than the dog excrement they just happened to step in. Even though discovering you've just stepped in dog poop right after telling yourself you've been insulted is bad enough, we'll see that their individual reactions can either make the situation infinitely worse or ameliorate their possibly hurt feelings.

Let's look at Sally's reaction. A few minutes after hearing the insult, Sally, the overly sensitive one, is now very upset. She's crying, her mascara running in black streams down her red cheeks, and she is vehemently blaming that person for hurting her feelings. She blames them for the poop she stepped in and for ruining the rest of her evening, and she insists they've ruined her whole life.

Is Sally correct? On Uranus, people would say yes and add that they too would be devastated if someone said something so mean, awful, and nasty to them.

But what do we see when we turn to look at Susie, the healthy twin? Susie merely shrugs and wipes her shoe on the grass before walking away. She's not crying and refuses to anger or upset herself. She goes on to enjoy the rest of her evening, and the thought that this little blip could possibly affect the rest of her life never even crosses her mind.

So how did the same situation cause such different reactions? Susie had the same mean, nasty things said to her that were said to her sister, but she had the exact opposite reaction. Let's see what each believed, what they told themselves—their self-talk—about the distasteful comments.

Sticks and Stones

Sally gasps at the attack, consequently giving herself a nice big whiff of what she just stepped in. With a small cry she looks at the bottom of her shoe, moaning when she sees the brown smear. And to top it off, she's convinced herself that they were her favorite pair of shoes, now utterly ruined and irreplaceable (maybe a bit of an exaggeration). Sally's eyes start to tear up as she thinks about the terrible insults. How can someone not like her? On top of that, they were so mean in their confrontation. "But what if they were right," a tiny voice in her head suggests. Maybe she *is* ugly and stupid. They didn't *have to* be so cruel and point it out, but if *they* believed it, then it *must* be true. And worse, she then thought, "That's it, the end. How can I ever overcome something as awful as that and find happiness?" Now, having settled into a serious crying jag, Sally believes that her life will suck, for eternity and then some. "No one will ever love me. I might as well give up now. It's so awful. Woe is me."

The poor thing, her thinking is from Uranus. She is making herself utterly miserable and doesn't have a clue that she is doing it. Sure, the mean, nasty words make it easy for her to think this way. They can influence her thinking if she chooses, but her self-talk is her responsibility. Other people's opinions and statements do not cause or control your feelings unless you are from Uranus. Others do not choose how you talk to yourself. *You* do. It's your choice.

Give Sally your credit card and tell her to go and buy this book. Her mind-set clearly could benefit from some major renovations.

Susie, on the other hand, blows it off. She believes the behavior was rude but does not insist on feeling insulted. Shrugging her shoulders, she thinks to herself, "Kiss my butt! Who do they think they are, anyway? Dung, schmung. It takes one to know one. Who cares what they think about me? That's their problem, not mine. It's only their opinion. I don't *need* their approval. I'll just go find people who do appreciate my company, people I enjoy being with." And she goes on her merry way, smiling and singing, "What they think about me is none of my business" (sung to the tune of "Zip-A-Dee-Doo-Dah"). It sounds like Susie has already bought this book!

If someone you tells you that you are ugly, they hate you, and you are a piece of crap, you could choose to use thinking from Uranus and tell yourself: "I'm no good. No one will ever love me. I'll be alone forever. It's so awful, I can't stand it." Telling yourself these things, especially believing them, will lead you to feel hurt and upset. And you will probably think it was the other person who made you feel that way. Now, you may not like what that person had to say, and most people would not, but you could instead choose to tell yourself, "What do they know? Even if they don't like me, it's not the end of the world. Yes, it's a hassle, but it's not horrible unless I make it so." You have choices about what you tell yourself. You could consider the source: "They are upset and angry." Or you could perhaps say to yourself, "They're deranged. What do they know?" and laugh about it. After all, they may be missing out on being with you. They don't know what an amazing person you are. And they are not even giving themselves the chance to know that amazing person, so consider it their loss, not yours. Are you getting the picture? You may not like it, but why *must* you upset yourself?

Remember that old saying, "Sticks and stones can break my bones, but words can never hurt me." Guess what? There's a lot of wisdom there! You are responsible for your feelings. Your partner is responsible for their own feelings. You can still be concerned about their feelings, however. But take note that you might be wasting your time by telling them that you are not responsible for their feelings when they are upset. Wait until things have cooled off. Instead, focus on your behavior, on your reaction. Avoid using their being upset as an excuse to focus on their "unfair" behavior and missing out on the opportunity to understand where they are coming from—what they are telling themselves about their own feelings.

The Gourmet Cake
Well, we've talked a lot about upsetting ourselves, but what about positive feelings? What about happiness—how does it come into play? On Uranus they believe that they can make other people happy. Do you think that you can make other people happy? Do you think someone could really make you happy? We knew you wouldn't fall for that one. You're catching on, right? Of course you can't make someone else happy. You might do something they like, but they still have a choice as to whether they will feel happy about it. That's right; it depends on what they tell themselves or what kind of a mood they are already in.

Example: You order a three-tier birthday cake from the most famous pastry chef in New York City, and you have it flown in for a surprise birthday party. The cake costs $2,000. This person is really special, and you want to show them that. You bring out the magnificent cake, and the birthday person takes a look at it, tastes it, and immediately says, "It's too sweet. The icing is the wrong color, and it's chocolate. You know I don't like chocolate cake." They sulk, blame you for ruining the party, and run off to the bedroom to cry. Do you think that you upset them?

If you insist, you could take responsibility for ruining their party. Yes, you tried to give them something really terrific and give them a really special party, but it didn't work. Why not? Who is responsible for the upset?

Here's a clue: It's not you! They upset themselves. Their expectations were off the wall, and so they had to think in terms of what you *should* or *should not* have done. "If you really loved me, you would know that I don't like my cake too sweet and that I don't like chocolate. Because you didn't love me enough to know my every wish and the picture in my head that I didn't share with you, it's obvious you don't love me at all, you SOB."

Well, it appears that you didn't realize just how self-centered and petty this person could act. You were erroneously expecting a thank-you, a smile, and even fond party memories...really fond. And by the way, those are relatively normal expectations. You may even have upset yourself and had the urge to "wring their neck until their eyeballs popped out," because you think they *shouldn't* act the way they are acting, which you think is immature."There's no pleasing them. Look at all I did—all the expense and great effort." You might be disappointed because of their response, but is it worth upsetting yourself over it? Maybe they are having a bad day. Or maybe that's just the way that person is? So maybe they *should* act that way because that's the way they act. Maybe you even learned a valuable lesson about using thinking from Uranus.

The Shake-and-Bake Cake
Now, maybe for their next birthday, or for someone else's, you decide that rather than going to all the trouble you went to last time only to get the results literally thrown back in your face, you will make a shake-and-bake cake. You know the kind; you nuke it in the microwave and spread some canned icing on it. Oops, it crumbles a little, and it's kind of crooked and uneven. Frankly, it's...well...kind of ugly. Oh well, hopefully it will do. You bring it out and present it to the birthday person and they say, "Wow. That was so nice of you. I'm so touched that you would go to all that trouble. Thank you! You've just made my day!" They don't know it only took six minutes. Your eyebrows rise in surprise and you smile. That was a very different reaction than the one before it.

Do you see that both birthday people had the option of telling themselves something disappointing or something happy? Think about how you feel when you tell yourself disappointing things.

That's right, you feel disappointed. Hey, it's your life, and it's up to you to choose what you tell yourself. With the skills you are learning in this book, you are already on your way to increasing your healthy thoughts and decreasing your upsetting thoughts from Uranus. It's pretty amazing, and we will bet you didn't think it would be so easy. Oops, we mean simple.

Do you see how you don't *have to* upset yourself? You can if you choose to, but you don't *have to*. You don't *have to* take it personally; it depends on what you tell yourself. It would be most unfortunate if you live for years believing that others make you happy, sad, angry, depressed, or guilty. Then you won't know you have a choice about what you choose to tell yourself, and you certainly would have great difficulty exercising the choice. Maybe you have lived that way for years, and perhaps you didn't know you had a choice. Well, now you do know, so you can think, plan ahead, and apply that knowledge as you go. Now that you know that thoughts cause and influence feelings, you can ask yourself, "Why *must* I upset myself just because you are angry and criticizing me? Why *must* I tell myself something upsetting?" The answer is: "I don't *have to*, and I am not going to." Hey, you might not be very fond of criticism, just as most people aren't, but even though you don't like it, you can draw the line and refuse to upset yourself about it: "I refuse to upset myself needlessly." With lots of practice, you can get better and better about refusing to upset yourself needlessly. People from Uranus are most always upsetting themselves needlessly because they don't know any other way. Work at trying not to think from Uranus.

If you have beliefs from Uranus, including poor self-acceptance, a truckload of *shoulds*, and the assumption that others cause and are responsible for your feelings, you will have a tendency to easily and frequently upset yourself needlessly. Now, we're not telling you that you *must not* upset yourself. You can choose to do it, if you wish. But why would you ever choose to? And it is a choice.

If Thoughts Cause Feelings, Why Not Just Recite Affirmations All Day Long and Be Happy All the Time?

Where do you think affirmations come from? We know that thoughts cause and influence feelings. Well, at some point, some brilliant person concluded, "I'll just tell myself positive stuff all day long, every day, whether it's accurate or not, and I'll always feel happy." If only it were that easy. We are hardly going to disagree that positive thoughts can lead to more positive feelings, but it is important to note that some things we face on a day-to-day basis may be negative and not in our best interest. These are best addressed as such. Remember, sometimes when things don't feel so good, this actually helps motivate us to make changes that may be in our best interest.

In the real world, there are some things we like and some things we don't like. So even though it may be nice to work at increasing your positive thinking, keep it reasonable. It's not necessary to completely delude yourself about reality or convince yourself that the world is completely wonderful or perfect. It's okay to "call 'em like you see 'em." It's not necessary to influence yourself unrealistically. And by the way, a little skepticism on occasion is actually healthy and frequently beneficial. After all, people are flawed and fallible. The important thing to note is that even though there are things around that you don't particularly like, you can still refuse to upset yourself about them while still maximizing your enjoyment of life. And above all, try to keep a good sense of humor. A good sense of humor is worth its weight in gold when it comes to positive mental health benefits.

If You Insist on Affirmations, Here Are Some Pretty Good Ones

You might try saying these affirmations to yourself in the morning as a little boost of strength to help you through the day. Think of them as your morning cup of positive-thinking coffee.

- To the best of my ability, I am going to make every effort to enjoy today.
- I am going to try to change the things that I don't like, if it is within my abilities.
- I am going to try to ignore the things that I can't change.
- I am going to do my best to think reasonably enough to make the best choice.
- I am going to decide if I am willing to try to change it or ignore it.
- I am going to try not to upset myself about the things that I have no control over.
- I am going to do my best to maintain the best sense of humor that I can.

Now you know where feelings come from. Thoughts cause and influence feelings.... Who would have ever believed it?

There may be some instances where feelings may appear to be unrelated to thoughts, such as in certain biochemical illnesses or other possible exceptions. And if push comes to shove, you might consider that thoughts at least have a significant effect or influence on feelings, if not directly causing them. The point, however, is to increase your self-responsibility and to help you focus on how and what you think, your self-talk, and how this relates to your feelings. In this regard, the assumption that thoughts cause feelings has great merit.

CHAPTER FIVE

Responsibility Versus Influence

PEOPLE FREQUENTLY ASK, "YOU mean other people can't hurt my feelings? But look what they did. Look what they said." The answer remains the same: most definitely not, even though it might seem like it because you are transferring responsibility and blaming them for your feelings. Others may do something you don't like. But when you demand that others *should not* do things you don't like and *should* do only things that you like, you are telling yourself something that is unreasonable. We all have individual responsibility, meaning none of us have the power to completely control another person. So it's futile to upset yourself when you can't control the actions of others. The only things you can fully control are your own actions and reactions. You are still responsible for your own thoughts about whatever it was that they did or didn't do. You are responsible for what you choose to tell yourself about their behavior. Your thoughts, including your conclusions, interpretations, and assumptions, cause and influence your feelings.

Influencing Others

Remember, however, that you may influence the thinking of others. Labeling someone by calling them a jerk makes it easier for them to upset themselves. Likewise, upsetting yourself becomes easier, or at least more tempting, if someone has labeled you and called you a jerk. So by all means take responsibility, consider that labeling yourself or others is an unhealthy habit. Just because others are responsible for their own feelings it does not necessarily mean that you can go around behaving inconsiderately, rudely, crudely, or in an infantile manner.

You are learning to use the basic tools for making healthy choices for yourself. Most people know that behaviors are choices and have consequences. But few know that how they think is a choice, and that unhealthy thinking has consequences. Those consequences are needless upset.

When you talk about responsibility for hurt feelings with a person who has been in therapy, they usually respond: "That's right. No one can hurt my feelings unless I let them." That's inaccurate, and, unfortunately, it's not that simple. The process of hurting feelings is not a passive one. You aren't just *letting* or giving another person permission to hurt your feelings. Thinking that your feelings are hurt requires a certain amount of work. Yes, you can think irrationally, upset yourself, and choose to hurt your feelings. But try not to kid yourself into believing that you if you are in that position that you can passively *let someone* hurt your feelings. You actively hurt your own feelings. They can't do it; only you can. It hardly makes sense that you could or would passively sit there and *let them* hurt your feelings. How you feel is your active responsibility—it is up to you. You do the same amount of work to hurt your feelings as it takes to instruct yourself not to hurt your feelings. You have a choice. This will take *work*!

If you have a tendency to hurt your own feelings or upset yourself needlessly, you have developed an unhealthy habit from Uranus. Sometimes you might even make excuses for this habit: "I'm sensitive...my feelings are easily hurt." Some may be more sensitive than others, but in the end, it is your brain, and everyone is personally responsible for their own thoughts, feelings, and behaviors.

Who Pushed the Button?

Did you ever say, "They pushed my buttons" or "They really know how to push my buttons?" If you really think someone else can push your buttons and *cause* you to feel a certain way, then we have a bridge across some prime (swamp) land we want to sell you (and that is not a good thing). If you were to say, "They have figured out the things they can say or do that I upset myself about," then we might believe you. You may be extra sensitive to certain things—usually criticism, perceived criticism, or rejection. But it's your own thoughts that fuel the upset.

When people talk about buttons, they are often talking about their leftover reactions as habitual thoughts about something that bothered them when they were growing up or sometime in the past. It may be related to some interaction between them and their parents; it's an interaction that they weren't very fond of, to say the least. It may be related to distress, upset, or pain, frequently from criticism or rejection, and is subsequently related to some very negative feelings. You might wonder why people are generally so sensitive to criticism and disapproval from others. When most of us were growing up, criticism equaled rejection, and you might remember that rejection didn't feel good but felt like a penalty. Our brains just aren't very fond of punishment, and most people aren't particularly fond of disapproval, rejection, or criticism.

By the way, buttons are hard to fix because they usually have been there a long time and have become incredible emotional liabilities. They require lots of time and effort to subdue! Identify them, challenge them, and replace them with healthy thinking! (See Exercise 5-2, "Changing Unhealthy Thinking," in Appendix II, "Exercises.")

Of course, you have probably already noticed that making someone else responsible for your "buttons" is the same as making that person responsible for your feelings. Enough said!

Ouch!

Did you ever hear someone say after breaking up with someone, "They really hurt me?" It's an all-too-common statement. In reality, you actually hurt yourself, because you gave the relationship value. Whether you are aware of doing so or not, you made a choice. If you did not value it, then there probably would be little or no pain. You chose to give the relationship value and bond with that person. When you choose to get involved in a relationship, you are gambling that the relationship will last forever. You already know that on Uranus the odds of it lasting are about fifty-fifty on a good day.

Are you ready to gamble? After all, if you bond but the relationship doesn't last, then there is a high likelihood that you are going to have some pain to deal with, some grieving. You chose to form this bond, and that decision will have a significant effect on how you feel later on in the relationship. Pay attention, and look both ways before you cross the road! You are the one voluntarily making the choice. No one is forcing you. You are responsible for the outcomes of your choices. Take responsibility for gambling on the relationship to start with. Accept that it might not work out; the bond might break, and yes, if that happens, there most likely will be hurt. If you are going to gamble, it's best that you take responsibility for your loss. After all, your brain's desire for pleasure isn't the casino's fault.

Perhaps you chose poorly. Perhaps you were lied to. Perhaps you were on the rebound. Well, you are still responsible for your choices and the consequences of those choices. They may all seem like poor choices, but nevertheless they are *your* choices. You are also responsible for all of your misperceptions. That means you might want to consider engaging in a little more scrutiny when you are choosing a partner. If you fail to ferret out the *shoulds*, irrational beliefs, mistruths, white lies, deception, and downright pathological lying, it is still *your* responsibility. It is you who bears the consequences of your choices. So when you are picking and choosing, keep your eyes and ears open and use healthy skepticism. But if you do happen to make a poor choice or a downright terrible blunder that you don't want to live with until eternity, then admit it, learn from it...and consider the benefits of cutting your losses and moving on.

Bonding, a Powerful Emotional Glue

A lot of the examples we have presented so far to help you learn the association between thoughts and feelings have not been examples of intimate relationships. You may have already noticed and thought, "It isn't that easy when it comes to dealing with my spouse, boy-/girlfriend, or longtime partner." Do you remember all the positive thoughts you had about them when you first met them? Do you remember how you ignored and refused to address any negatives? Do you remember the wonderful positive feelings that were generated by all of that positive thinking? Isn't being in love grand, all awash with positive thoughts and emotions? Well, when you are bonding with all the happy thoughts and are logging in all of those positive feelings, it does feel great.

Guess what happens when it's over. Each one of those happy thoughts and feelings then requires a payout in negative thoughts and feelings. You lost them all in the poker game of your relationship, and it doesn't feel too good to *have to* return all of your previous winnings. Guess what happens when once-trickling negative emotions erupt and spew forth like a volcano as you are breaking the bond. You get to deal with the ol' broken heart...ugh...incredible pain...gut-wrenching pain...pain that feels overwhelming. Falling out of love and breaking the bond comes with the same intense flood of feelings as in the beginning, but they are now of opposite quality: intense, miserable grief—a hurricane of negative feelings.

When relationships begin, bonding is related to the amount of time spent together or spent thinking positively about each other. During this time you are recording all of the positive thoughts and feelings you are enjoying: the great laughs, great food, warm touches and caresses, great sex, more great sex...all multiplied by wonderful thoughts. However, real intimacy, really knowing and liking that partner, is typically scarce to nonexistent. You haven't gotten to know everything about your partner.

Traditionally negative perceptions are ignored and the partner is placed on a pedestal of wonderful pretenses. So you really don't know them. Pretending eventually gives way to reality at some point and to the harsh realization that there are flaws and traits that we don't like. As we get to know the partner, and if the negatives eventually outweigh the positives, it becomes, "I love them, but I'm not in love with them." That is a very popular refrain when the love has worn thin. You have "had it up to here."

In other words, you are bonded to them, but you really don't much *like them* anymore. You might consider this as a more reasonable definition for love: "I'm bonded to them and I like them." Don't confuse bonding with love. Love is not just being bonded to someone. It also includes *liking* the person; it is caring about them, including being concerned about how they feel. Have you ever been apart from someone and missed them? Just because you miss someone, it doesn't mean that you love them. It means that you are bonded to them.

Most relationships reach some compromise in the middle between the two extremes of wonderful and awful, between being in love and out of love. Relationships tend to reach this middle-of-the-road compromise as the difficulty of dealing with the reality of each other's fallibility becomes more apparent, also known as when "the honeymoon is over." This divergence usually creates a relationship rut down the middle caused by each person moving a safe distance away—not close enough to risk the pain of rejection, but also not far enough away to feel the bond breaking. A wall is formed to avoid painful feelings. This safe distance tends to endure until it slowly gives way to the realization of the underlying misery. It is either perpetuated for eternity or culminates in the throes of divorce.

Why Are Conflicts Harder to Resolve Once I Am Bonded?

Normal everyday differences of opinion are usually the easiest to resolve. However, after bonding has taken place, significant conflicts in relationships frequently occur because one of the parties feels slighted or rejected. Disagreements are more difficult to deal with in bonded relationships because the emotional stakes are higher, owing to the potential pain of increased distance and—heaven forbid—a broken heart. Pain is on the line, so it's hard to negotiate compromises in the middle, especially when rigid, irrational, polarized thinking prevails, when wonderful versus awful, being "in love" versus being "out of love," is present. It's very important to address these relationship issues in a healthy and reasonable way early on, so that you will have a much better chance of maintaining a healthy long-term relationship.

There are two parts to feeling hurt or rejected. One is the actual event, and the other is the conclusion drawn about the event. For example, your partner may do something that you perceive as wrong, unfair, unjust, or just plain dumb. They may have forgotten your birthday. Maybe they didn't listen when you wanted to share something that seemed very important to you, or maybe they just generally ignored you. They may have voiced disapproval in an unhealthy way. These are actual slights or rejections. Be careful of the conclusions you draw about them, though. Your conclusions will significantly influence your perception and likely distort the reality of the situation. It may be bad enough to be ignored, which is the *actual* slight or rejection, but you don't *have to* make it worse by assuming a negative conclusion about the motive behind the action.

You make it worse by concluding that it means you are unloved, you are uncared-for, and you are no good. Jumping to conclusions is almost always a mistake. The reasonable person will take responsibility for addressing the complaint with their partner rather than jumping to a conclusion that might be erroneous. They will let their partner know that they do not like it when the partner does whatever *it* is. They forgot your birthday? Sure, you would really like it if they remembered your birthday. After all, you always remember theirs. But try not to overgeneralize and jump to the conclusion that they don't love you, that you are unlovable, or that they are a total jerk... unless you are hell-bent on upsetting yourself needlessly.

Inevitably, you will sometimes jump to conclusions. Humans do that. When you express your dislike to your partner, try to take responsibility for your hurt. Here is an example: "I did not like it when you came home late and didn't call to tell me. I told myself that you probably don't care about me or don't love me when you act so inconsiderately. I felt distant and hurt." This would at least be an appropriate way to express this dislike.

However, it may take a lot of practice for you to achieve anything close to this, especially if there has been a growing series or history of behaviors that you believe are inconsiderate.

Did you notice that in the example the person took responsibility for their dislikes and their feelings? It certainly would be nice and very important if the alleged offending partner would express concern about their partner's reaction. This does not mean they are taking responsibility for it, however. It just means they acknowledge it and are willing to apologize. Here is an example of that kind of response: "I can see you feel hurt, and I apologize for not calling you when I knew I was going to be late. I agree that it would have been better if I had called. I'll work on it and make every effort to call the next time if I'm going to be late."

This type of direct communication leads to real and healthy exchanges that would never happen on Uranus. There is no blaming and no fault placed on anyone's *shoulds*. Neither participant is attacked as being a "bad guy." The healthy reassurance lays out a reasonable plan to work on "fixing things" and avoids the building of walls. On Uranus there are miles of walls, very thick, high walls that are frequently impenetrable. By apologizing and offering reasonable reassurance, the late person in our scenario avoided the pitfalls of Uranus, where bestowing fault and blaming prevail. No time was wasted arguing, and no marathon was conducted to talk about feelings and injustice ad nauseam. There was no long list dating back years that had to be covered until the wee hours of the morning. The feelings were addressed with concern for those feelings but without taking responsibility for the other person's feelings.

It is important that you are concerned about your partner's feelings and demonstrate that concern. It is equally important, however, that you don't take responsibility for those feelings. This may take some practice, however, because obviously people don't like feeling rejected or hurt. Therefore, your being reasonable during these circumstances is important and may require great effort on your part.

Drawing the Line: I Don't Like It, but I'm Not Going to Upset Myself About It!

Take note, there is a big difference between not liking something and upsetting yourself about it. On Uranus they don't know that there is a difference and they routinely upset themselves needlessly. They don't know that they have a choice about what they tell themselves. Stop and think a minute. You don't upset yourself every time something happens that you don't like. For example, let's say that your partner asks you to go to the bank or the grocery store. You don't really want to go, but you go anyway. When you get there it is really busy, and you're having a hell of a time getting out of there. So you look around for the shortest line. Unfortunately, it is the busiest part of the week, and all of the lines stretch back for what seems like miles. Sure, you might mumble and grumble and be annoyed, but you will probably suck it up like the rest of us poor slobs and stand in line. You might swear to yourself to get an ATM card, bank by computer, or never, ever shop at this time of day again. You don't like it. You feel miffed, but you cope and blow it off. If someone asked you why you didn't upset yourself, you would likely reply, "It just didn't seem worth it." Guess what. It rarely, if ever, is worth it.

You could make yourself upset and go ballistic by telling yourself how awful, terrible, and unfair it is, and what a louse your partner is for making you go (actually, *you* chose to go). But that wouldn't shorten the lines, and it would probably make you feel worse. Thinking from Uranus and upsetting yourself is an easy way to make a bad situation worse. It only compounds the problem. You then have the original problem, the long line, as well as the second problem, the upset you have caused yourself. Hopefully, you don't create a third problem by behaving stupidly in a way that might get you thrown out the door or arrested. The upset is needless and unproductive. Work on gaining control over the needless upset by taking responsibility for your self-talk and emotions. Work on minimizing or perhaps eliminating the needless upset.

Identifying Self-Talk From Uranus
Learn to identify your self-talk from Uranus. People usually have great difficulty identifying irrational, unhealthy, and inaccurate self-talk. Look out for labeling and self-rating. Look for the *shoulds*. Look for "awfulizing" and dramatic overgeneralizations and blaming. If you are feeling upset, your self-talk is probably negative and unhealthy. Take notice and search it out. Learn to ask yourself the following questions:

1 **What am I telling myself?** What you are telling yourself is your self-talk. Work on learning to identify your self-talk. It is a very good idea to write down your self-talk, because you can easily trick yourself. Try keeping a journal of your self-talk, and especially, the unhealthy self-talk that you use to upset yourself. Each time it is unhealthy, note when it happened and what you were telling yourself. Try to avoid censoring anything. If you like, you can also write down what you were doing when it started and see how you could think about the situation differently. This will help you begin to notice and monitor your self-talk by making it something tangible you can refer back to and work on through writing about it.
2 **Does it make sense?** Look at each statement and conclusion you recorded. Does it really make sense? Is it really believable?

3 **Where's the proof?** Just because you think something is so, that doesn't make it accurate. Try to find evidence or lack of evidence to support or refute your belief, especially if you upset yourself with it. Now, it is usually best if you try to avoid fabricating proof. Be careful and vigilant. When you are thinking from Uranus, you are more likely to try to fool yourself. And just because you feel a certain way, it does not make those feelings proof that what you believe is true. If you are still in doubt, go back and review the basic assumptions in Chapter 1 ("I Love You. You're Perfect. Now Change!")...no labeling or self-rating allowed. "Am I telling myself something irrational? Am I thinking from Uranus?"
4 **Do I have a choice about what I tell myself?** You know the answer to that one. Of course you have a choice.

In the rest of this book you will learn how to use these skills to improve your life and relationships. Are you beginning to see how Paul and Barbara were short on reasonable thinking? How they were thinking from Uranus? There was a lack of self-acceptance, a ton of *should*-ing, and a significant amount of blaming the other person for their own feelings. Each avoided taking responsibility for their own thoughts, feelings, and behaviors...for their own happiness. Their unhealthy thinking from Uranus rendered them helpless and unable to resolve their relationship problems. If they had been thinking more reasonably, expressing their likes and dislikes in healthier ways, they might be lounging on a beach in Hawaii right now instead of arguing at the marriage counselor's office.

Are you beginning to see what we mean by changing the process? If you change the way you think, then you have the ability to change other things in the relationship. But if you don't change your unhealthy thinking and replace it with a healthier thinking process, you're unlikely to maximize your relationship's success. On Uranus they don't take responsibility for their own thoughts, their own feelings, or their own behaviors. Instead, they insist that others are responsible.

It doesn't take a rocket scientist to realize that unhealthy thinking produces unhealthy results. Having misconceptions about the origin of feelings has a long-term eroding effect on relationships, potentially leading to their demise.

CHAPTER SIX

Is It Love, or What?

LET'S LOOK BACK ONCE again at our unhappy twin from earlier, Sally. Once upon a time on Uranus, despite all of her insecurities, Sally was in fact a very nice young girl, well behaved and popular among her peers. In junior high school she began to notice boys. She experienced that initial spark of curiosity about those previous carriers of the incredibly infectious disease known as "cooties," and they began to seem less and less icky. They began to seem rather cute, maybe even worth taking a second glance at. The old playground dirt seemed to have disappeared from their faces, hands, and knees, revealing surprisingly attractive creatures (dare we say humans?) underneath. This did not, of course, change Sally's model behavior in any way. As you might remember, Sally is too immersed in Uranian culture to not strive for absolute (and impossible) perfection in everything she does. She missed very little school, and then only when it was a legitimate medical illness with a note from her doctor. She did as she was told and lived the good life. Sally joined the cheerleading squad along with her sister, gaining entrance to the elite popular crowd. She was friendly with all her fellow students, though, and so was welcome and pretty much well liked in all circles. In high school Sally began to date, and she continued to date throughout. She was the envy of all when the quarterback, a tall Adonis-like young man, asked her to their senior prom. She continued to date in college, and not just the athletes. Her sophomore year, she became smitten with a rock guitar player, dutifully attending every one of his band's concerts (although there weren't all that many). During her senior year a soft-spoken writer won her over with his poems. But it seemed that no matter how nice she was, no matter how hard she tried to look pretty, be caring, or do what she could to make the relationship work, none of her boyfriends worked out. She always ended up getting the worst of it; she was always the one who ended up with the broken heart. She discovered the musician was paying lip service, literally, to some of his groupies, and the writer announced one day about six months into the relationship that she no longer inspired him and that he had found another muse. Sally seemed forever doomed to pick the "wrong" guy. In a nutshell, all her love relationships bombed.

It would seem that Sally wasn't in school the day they taught "How to Pick 'Em 101." Is she doomed to be forever alone, maybe one day find that she has become the spinster aunt with 10-plus cats? Maybe not. Do you know how the majority of people on Uranus pick their partners? Do you know how *you* picked your partner? Most people don't. They too were out sick when "How to Pick 'Em 101" was taught.

One poor man suffering from the same malady as Sally claimed he was just really choosy. "I only go out with special women," he once boasted to several friends who were sitting around drinking with him one night. "Yeah, right," they laughed. "You only go out with those women who dare to go out with you." Unfortunately, his friends weren't buying his excuse, one that is used all too often in cases like this.

It seems that a great many people think they are choosy when it comes to picking a partner. They think they are in control of choosing a partner. Most fail to realize how many things actually influence their decision.

Do you remember the fairy tales and nursery rhymes where the wonderful prince or the dashing white knight happened by and snatched the damsel from distress, and the two of them proceeded to live happily ever after? Don't you just wish that were true? Have you been waiting and searching for that perfect white knight to come and rescue you from all the dating madness? Guess what? Some goofball from Uranus made up those silly stories, and of course you fell for them. It would be great if things in real life went that way, and for all we know, on rare occasion they might. But let's just say the likelihood is very, very low. You'll probably win the million-dollar lottery two weeks in a row, see pigs fly, and discover the lost city of Atlantis before it happens.

There is a lot that influences how we select partners. How about the influence of music, poetry, movies, television, fairy tales, and all those articles in magazines? Take a minute and really listen to the lyrics to some hit songs, past or present. There are some real horsefeathers in there. As we listen and read, we start believing some of that ballyhoo and blather.

You are probably aware that people are frequently drawn to one another because of their looks, their physical appearance. Is it love or what? Is it real? Will it last? There are a lot of handsome guys and beautiful women out there who can eventually act like jerks. It generally takes time to get to know someone. And once you really get to know them, the big question is, do you still like them? All too often the answer is no. You might phrase it this way: "I still love them, but I am not *in* love with them" or "The thrill is gone." What you might really mean is: "He acts like a jerk." The prince turned out to be a frog. But then you might think, "I am bonded to him, and it will hurt too much to leave." People frequently make the mistake of "bonding" to the person before they really get to know them. It may sound silly, but it happens pretty regularly. This is just a guess: Did the light bulb just flash on, and are you now nodding your head? Are you holding your head at the same time? Are you saying, "No! No! Not me!" Well, keep listening, because Mr. or Ms. Pretty on the Outside but Feeling Ugly on the Inside is not the only person you might want to watch out for.

Have you ever had a persistent suitor, the person who is always in the wings, always available, and doesn't take no for an answer? No, not the stalker! We're talking about the friend, the coworker, the classmate who you know wants to be with you— all the time. Maybe they tolerate a lot from you. Maybe they hang around even when you have someone else. They are just "always there"—always the good listener or providing the shoulder for you to cry on. You thought, "Awww, now isn't that sweet"; maybe you've thought that it was time you gave them a chance. Well, beware and look before you leap. Sometimes this kind of persistence is interpreted as true love when it turns out to actually be plain old run-of-the-mill neediness. We're not suggesting you now avoid this person, but you might consider steering clear of making them your next romantic partner.

Beware of a lot of sweet-smelling flowers early on. These are the ones who don't even know you yet, but they "just know" that you are the one. They are a real fireball that comes on really strong. They put a lot of energy into the relationship, and they sweep you off your feet. What chemistry! It has to be love at first sight! It feels so good when you are around them...and so bad when you're not. They text you six times a day, especially when "our song" is playing on the radio. Then there are the phone calls you *have to* exchange with them another 106 times a day. Wow, the passion, the excitement...the excessiveness...this *must* be love, right? Hmmm, you might want to take a step back for a minute and take a good hard look at this quickly budding relationship.

Maybe it is just lust. Maybe it is neediness. Is it love, or what? Maybe it's "or what." It is up to you to analyze the situation and draw your own conclusion.

And, hey, if it is just lust, maybe that's okay with you. There is nothing inherently wrong with lust. Play your cards right, and you might make it last a while. But is it the only basis for what could become a long-lasting relationship, whether pleasant or unpleasant? Figuring that out may be difficult and painful, but doing it now rather than, say, after you've gotten married is likely to be far less of an emotional nightmare. Good luck. Be careful of the snow job—not from them but from you! Be careful of what you are telling yourself. We humans have the amazing ability to talk ourselves into almost anything, including relationships that are built on figurative "flying pigs." If it sounds like neediness or control, run like hell! If it sounds too good to be true, be suspicious. It usually is.

Hints on How to Pick 'Em
When you meet someone interesting, start with healthy skepticism. How can skepticism be healthy? Well, first of all, it demonstrates that you recognize you are a flawed and fallible human being in a world that is sometimes unpredictable and full of other flawed and fallible humans. Healthy skepticism helps you pick them, but of course it does not guarantee you will get the perfect mate. However, increasing the intensity of your scrutiny allows you to optimize your chances of making a more accurate choice. Healthy skepticism is incompatible with blind infatuation and overestimation of a person's relationship value.

It is okay to think someone is generally great, wonderful, or terrific. In other words, they have a lot of qualities you like, but be skeptical. Don't forget that they are human. Yes, this means they are flawed and fallible. They can have good days and bad days, good traits and bad traits, things you like and things you don't like. Try not to get yourself bonded to someone prematurely and then convince yourself that you are in love. Take a good hard look first. On Uranus people get hooked on blind faith and their own gullible assumptions. They forget or don't know how to use healthy skepticism.

Have a Reasonable Definition of Love
On Uranus love is seen as that feeling we believe we *should* have for someone or something. We *should* love our mother, apple pie, our children, and so on. We may not like them, let alone love them, but we keep telling ourselves we are *supposed* to. *Morally*, we are *supposed* to because it is the *right* thing to do and *good people* do that. When we apply this kind of love definition to our relationships, it can leave us in great trouble. We might tell ourselves that we *have to* love them because we married them, we slept with them, the planets were aligned when we met them, or our horoscope signs are compatible with theirs. Are you getting the drift, or do you want a few more silly reasons? We can also tell ourselves that they *have to* love us for the same silly reasons.

Healthy love, on the other hand, is what we had best apply to our relationships. Healthy love is when someone meets the vast majority of our physical, emotional, psychological, and behavioral preferences, not our *needs*. Then the resulting feeling is called love.

When we don't use healthy skepticism, there is a greater possibility that when we think we are falling in healthy love, we are in fact succumbing to "Uranus love." (No, that isn't a hit song from the past.) You like the person. You enjoy them, you feel generally positive about them, and you may even be willing to risk bonding with them. On the other hand, when they stop meeting those preferences, you no longer feel love toward them.

You don't much want to even be around them. And by that point you may have "had it up to here" and probably have compiled a long list of their transgressions. You might even "hate their guts" and are ready to march to your front door, fling it open, and yell, "Get the hell out." When they stop meeting your preferences, you generally feel negative toward them. It seems like the positives have decreased and the negatives have increased. "I love them, but I'm not in love with them." Yeah, right—we already know what that means: The honeymoon stage is definitely over. You may even be motivated to end the relationship and break the bond at this point.

How many times have people thought they were in love because the other person was good-looking, persistent, passionate, or treated them "special"? They never argue with you. They never criticize you, and they always "make" you feel good. They are always very reassuring and attentive. They say and act like they *need* you. And no matter how many other people told you to be careful, slow down, stay away, or run like hell, you were "blinded by love"? Come on. We know people change, but were you ever paying attention to those early clues, the road signs and traffic lights? Did you ever use any healthy skepticism? Did you ever assess their relationship skills or your own? Did you ever really look objectively at compatibility, or take an objective look at your preferences in the physical, psychological, or behavioral areas and see how they matched the other person? Did you look for their pluses and their minuses? Or did you give yourself a mental snow job and talk yourself into *falling* in love?

Remember, others don't make you fall in love. *You* make yourself fall in love. It's an active process related to what you are telling yourself about the other person. People only fall blindly in love on Uranus...with their eyes closed. You remember, "love is blind." For healthy skepticism, you are required to open your eyes, keep them wide open, and resist the urge to look away every now and then. That is, you examine the potential of the relationship from your illuminated perspective with as much insight as possible.

You have a better chance of picking wisely if you have a plan. Ponder this: There was a guy who put together a questionnaire he gave to women whenever he was at a bar, lounge, singles gathering, or other social event. He asked a lot of personal questions. He did it as an icebreaker, never really expecting anyone to fill it out. He found out, though, that it was a terrific icebreaker, and some people were actually offended that he didn't give them one. A lot of the women wanted to know how they scored. Maybe this was the basis for personal ads and dating web sites? What a great system! You tell someone what you are looking for, and hopefully, the matches respond and the nonmatches don't respond. It would be nice if it really worked that way. Some of those dating sites may actually attempt this, but unfortunately, potential suitors still tend to fudge what they tell you.

Whether it's intentional or unintentional, people don't always express themselves in a straightforward manner. They might tell you what they think you want to hear. Over time, you may even find that their opinion of themselves differs greatly from your opinion of them. So develop your own plan to evaluate them, and put some healthy skepticism into it. By now you are hopefully getting better at realizing the importance of taking into account our human imperfection. Yes, let's repeat it together: "We are all flawed and fallible." Healthy skepticism improves the odds of getting to know someone. It is okay to ask questions, but remember it may take some time to *really* get to know somebody. So be careful about spending too much time with them or committing to an exclusive relationship until you have had time to develop a more accurate appraisal of them.

When you are getting to know someone, don't just ask about their preferences, their likes and dislikes. Observe their behaviors. Be on the alert for *shoulds* and other signs of rigid thinking from Uranus. Learn to express your likes and dislikes as preferences and opinions... rather than dogmatic, rigid rules or eleventh and twelfth commandments.

Ask perspective partners their opinions, especially their opinions about relationships and relationship skills. Yes, they might say what they think you want to hear, but it can also be a tip-off if it is expressed in dogmatic *shoulds, musts,* and *have to*'s. The real test, the one to pay special attention to, is when you disagree. If, in the early stages, you can't agree to disagree, then there will be trouble. If you or your potential partner thinks the two of you *must* agree on everything, then this has the makings of a poor match. This is because two people who believe they *must* always agree will spend a lot of time avoiding talking about important differences of opinions. They will probably be unable to provide reasonable criticism that is very helpful in relationship problem solving.

Be a good detective and look for clues. What kind of temperament do they have? Is it one you could live with, possibly forever? Are they reliable? Do they keep commitments? Do they generally do what they say they are going to do? Do they say what they mean and mean what they say? How do they treat others? This can be a tip-off if they rate and label people and see themselves as superior or inferior to others. By all means, try to avoid making gullible assumptions from Uranus.

Gravitate Toward the Traits of a Healthy Partner
Healthy partners demonstrate

- A desire to evaluate and express views as opinions, especially as likes and dislikes.
- Flexibility... "I would prefer" rather than "I *need* or *have to.*"
- Integrity... straightforwardness with reliability and dependability.

- Straightforwardness...but tempered with tactfulness. Remember, it's an opinion.
- Accurate communication...done openly and freely without defensiveness. Mean what you say and say what you mean.
- Healthy independence...you are not joined at the hip. You were an individual before you started the relationship, and you are still one. You now just have areas of overlap, mutual interests.
- Willingness to compromise...reasonableness
- Concern and consideration for the other's well-being...including their likes and dislikes
- Sense of humor and ability to laugh at themselves
- Responsibility...each partner takes responsibility for their own thoughts, feelings, and behaviors while letting the other person take responsibility for their own
- Self-acceptance, with a willingness to listen to others' viewpoints and opinions
- Willingness to work on incorporating healthier rules and communication in the relationship

Watch Out for the Traits of an Unhealthy Partner
Unhealthy partners demonstrate

- An inability to express their views and opinions as anything other than "right" or "wrong."
- Rigid thinking and expectations...*should, must, have to.* They express likes and dislikes as demands.
- Lack of integrity, reliability, and dependability.
- Dishonesty or "brutal honesty."
- Inaccurate communication that is guarded and defensive.
- Unhealthy and excessive dependence and neediness.
- Unwillingness to compromise or be reasonable.
- A general lack of concern and consideration for the other's well-being, including their opinions.

- A lack of humor and an inability to laugh at themselves.
- A desire to blame others, along with a lack of responsibility for their own individual thoughts, feelings, and behaviors.
- Labeling and rating, with an unwillingness to listen to the other's viewpoints and opinions.
- Unwillingness or outright refusal to work on incorporating healthier rules and communication in the relationship.

Make Your Own List of What You Are Looking for in a Partner
Put together a list of what you want in a partner: the characteristics you prefer in one column and the characteristics that are unacceptable in another. Rate each item on a scale of 1 to 10, where 1 = not very important, 5 = moderately important, and 10 = very important. When interacting with prospective partners, remember to keep your healthy skepticism. Try not to rationalize problems away and get so caught up in the excitement of newness that you turn a blind eye. Try to be reasonable, but don't ignore characteristics that you think are deal-breakers.

We previously mentioned that criticism is frequently avoided early on in relationships—so as not to sink the "love boat." New couples avoid it much the same way that people avoid being exposed to the plague, kicking small animals, and picking their nose or scratching in certain places in public. If you learn to express your preferences in terms of likes and dislikes, and especially if you have learned to address the behavior instead of the person, then make it a point to practice this early on in the relationship. Observe whether your partner reciprocates. How partners handle criticism, complaints, and differences of opinion can ultimately influence the outcome of the relationship. How are your skills in these areas? Do you think you would benefit from a little more practice?

Try not to be fooled into thinking that everything is wonderful just because no one ever complains or argues. Be especially concerned if you hear yourself saying, "We never argue." Life presents conflicts and differences of opinions in most all relationships. Complaints are frequently there but not expressed. It is important to discuss the complaints so they can be dealt with and not swept under the rug. If you sweep them under the rug, don't be surprised when they cause lumps that add up and trip you later on. The point is not necessarily whether complaints exist but how skillfully they are dealt with. It is important to have reliable conflict-resolution skills. When conflicts arise, the key is how the complaining or criticism is expressed and handled. Do you become defensive? Do they become defensive? If so, you can change it. Work on it. Hopefully you are already working on making improvements. Check to see if your partner is also willing to work on it.

Handling Defensiveness
When you are trying to work on your own sensitivity, try to look for "that feeling you get" when you feel criticized and react with defensiveness. Look for defensive behavior when you feel you *must* justify your position. When you get the feeling that you are being attacked, refuse to get defensive, a reaction that likely has already become almost automatic. Like other suggestions for things to work on in this book, this will take some work, and very possibly a lot of work. If you do get the urge to act defensively, you could try counting to three, five, or whatever other number works for you before responding. This can give you a little emotional space in which to step back, calm down, and actively think rather than reacting habitually on autopilot.

There is no law that says you *must* defend yourself. Why *must* you defend yourself? Instead, focus on the other person's complaint or position. Take this as an opportunity to hone your listening skills. Perhaps you can learn something valuable about your flawed and fallible self? There may be some instances when explaining your position is reasonable. If you learn not to automatically go into the defensive mode, you then have the option of explaining yourself if it is appropriate. Making this distinction will take a good deal of work. It's hard to break old habits of automatically reacting to our emotions. Most people don't like disapproval. It is a form of rejection that doesn't feel very pleasant. However, we can learn to choose better ways to respond to these unpleasant feelings.

Try not to avoid expressing yourself because you "don't want to hurt their feelings." If you still believe that silliness at this point, go back and reread the first few chapters, maybe even several times! And if the other person is fearful of hurting your feelings, then it is your job to let them know that "only I can hurt my feelings." Express your belief that the relationship will be a lot better off if you both practice taking responsibility for your own thoughts, feelings, and behaviors. Practice expressing your criticisms as opinions and preferences, and not rigid *rights* and *wrongs* riddled with *should, must, need to, have to,* etc.

If someone frequently discourages you from expressing your likes and dislikes or punishes you while you are trying to express them, be especially apprehensive. They are just opinions, just words. It is not as if you are physically threatening or hurting them, so a consistent extreme reaction or oppressive attempt to suppress them is definitely suspicious. If they try to control you or they fly into a rage, you might want to start questioning their motives, and you might suspect that their intentions are unlikely stemming from a desire to improve closeness by getting to know you better. You might instead conclude that they are trying to control you with one-way communication, blocking or eliminating your voice, rather than encouraging better two-way communication.

Check to see if you are expressing yourself in a healthy way and avoiding ineffective communication such as yelling, screaming, crying, throwing things, or making threats. If the other person chooses the latter method, it is reason for concern. When complaints are dealt with in a tantrum-like manner, the original message usually gets lost. Then the reaction typically winds up being to the angry reaction rather than the complaint. Be sure that you are expressing yourself in the healthiest way possible. If you are using appropriate and healthy skills to deliver your message in a reasonable manner, and your partner continues to discourage your expressing your opinions and preferences, then you have some serious decisions to make. At some point, you will face deciding whether the degree of unhealthy relating is acceptable to you and consider whether you have any other options, what they are, and which one best fits the situation. For example:

- Ask them if they are willing to work on improving their skills while you continue to focus on improving your skills.
- Ignore their lack of cooperation while you continue to work on improving your skills and refuse to disturb yourself about their unwillingness.
- Try not to forever upset yourself about their nonparticipation while insisting that they be different from the way they are.
- If you are telling yourself they *shouldn't* be that way, then guess what? They are that way. And if you prefer, you can continue to eternally upset yourself about it. But the fact remains, that is the way they behave.
- Decide if the relationship is in your best interest.

If you are already done with the picking process, have been together since dirt was invented, got married, have kids, have a ton of debt, or there is any other reason that you are already with someone and are hoping to make it work or improve on it—you know, already bonded—you can still do most of the things mentioned in this chapter. Give up the definitions of love from Uranus. Give up the belief from Uranus that "love will find a way...love conquers all...they are responsible for my feelings and my happiness...I *must* make them love me...if they really loved me...etc." *Should* I stay or *should* I go? Is it real or what?

CHAPTER SEVEN

The Wrath of Uranus

BARBARA STARED AT THE ceiling as she lay awake in bed. She clenched her jaw, fuming over the dismal results of her attempt at bringing some romance back into her and Paul's sad excuse for a marriage. Barbara felt like ripping apart the expensive negligee she had bought earlier that afternoon and was still wearing. It was either that or start sobbing. The night had started with Paul returning home late again; it seemed to be becoming a habit of his. The romantic candlelit dinner she'd planned on surprising him with had grown cold. She'd been sitting in front of her own untouched plate, nursing a glass of the expensive red wine she had also bought earlier that day, when Paul walked in the door. He claimed he'd needed to stay late working on some important project he was heading at the office, so he'd ended up ordering in food anyway. Barbara picked up their plates and headed to the kitchen to begin cleaning up. Paul's claim that it looked delicious and his pained look as she left did little to ease the tightly coiled knot of tension, anger, and hurt in her chest that had been slowly forming all evening.

A heavy silence descended at that point, Barbara continuing to clean up as if Paul wasn't even there. He decided to retire to their bedroom, shoulders slumped under the weighty guilt eating him up inside. What else could he do, though? Her expression as she'd left the dining room with their full dinner plates said loud and clear that she didn't want to hear anything else he might have to say in explanation or apology. So Paul figured he'd already dug himself a pretty deep hole, though he'd done so unintentionally, and he'd do better to just disappear and give her time to cool off. How was he supposed to have known she'd made plans for tonight? Rubbing his hands over his face in defeat and exhaustion, Paul decided to just get in bed and wait. He was almost asleep, unable to keep his eyes open after the long day at work, when he noticed Barbara go quietly into their bathroom. Barbara walked out a short while later, smiling seductively and wearing a silk negligée. Paul sighed, knowing that his body's demand for sleep—and his heavy eyelids assured him he didn't have much of a choice in the matter—was about to make things a whole lot worse.

Barbara posed by the bathroom door a minute, showing off the new silk negligée, before walking over to the bed and trying to look like the seductive siren that she really didn't feel like after her earlier disappointment. Paul's sigh as he looked up at her was followed by the whining explanation that he'd worked his tail off all day and was exhausted. He told her he was sorry and that she looked amazing, but he just couldn't keep his eyes open. That knot of sick tension in her chest grew, making it almost impossible to breathe. Okay, that was strike two, but she wasn't ready to give up just yet. As a last-ditch effort, Barbara slid into bed next to him, pulling his face down to hers, trying to coax any kind of response from him. After a minute Paul just pulled back, gave her another pained look, kissed her quickly, and murmured, "I love you." Then he proceeded to roll over and go to sleep. To Barbara, it felt like a punch to the gut. Her once warm, loving look faded into a piercing coldness that dismissed any hint of her heartbreak as she slumped back on the bed.

Barbara had now been lying awake staring at the ceiling for almost an hour, painful thoughts swirling around in her mind. The automatic smile she used to get when she looked into his eyes had disappeared somewhere along the line. She hated his distant and aloof demeanor. She was sick of him never considering her needs, feelings, desires. He was no longer caring or affectionate; everything she said seemed to just go in one ear and straight out the other. Feelings of defeat, humiliation, and worthlessness ate away at her, as did the gut-wrenching pain of rejection.

Paul's snoring broke into her thoughts. Barbara threw back the covers and glared at him sleeping peacefully next to her. She stormed out of their bedroom. Was she imagining things, or had the man she once loved just morphed into such a hateful monster that she couldn't even stand to lie next to him any longer? The fire that had burned so strongly at first seemed to have slowly diminished over the years. Tonight it felt different, as if it had been snuffed out, and she felt cold inside. She thought to herself, "Where did all the love go?" The thought of leaving him crept in, but with it came intense, jarring pain. If it hurt so much to even think about leaving, then that had to mean she still loved him. "So why am I so miserable when we're together? I'm not sure I even like him anymore," Barbara thought sadly, as she was sinking down onto the couch in their living room. With a sigh, she slumped forward, cradling her head in her hands.

Here Is How It Began

Initially, Paul and Barbara met and were infatuated with each other as a result of mutual physical attraction and a flood of positive thoughts about each other. Their attraction led to the illusion of falling in love and a premature choice. Compliments, good behavior, hugs, kisses, smiles, laughter, and a honeymoon atmosphere originally dominated the relationship. The bonding was beginning and criticism was taboo.

This positive-only attitude created an unrealistic imbalance by inhibiting the potential ability of both to perceive the good, the bad, and the sometimes ugly qualities of each other. It resulted in a pseudo-closeness, or a falsely positive relationship, where complaints were suppressed. This was the start of a polarized, black-and-white relationship that ultimately shifted from wonderful to awful. The fall off the pedestal, the fall from grace, was a relationship disaster. The participants worked hard to magnify the positives. They worked equally hard to ignore the negatives. They pretended as much and as often as they could... hey, it feels so good! During this time the bond was being cemented between them, but communication errors were piling up.

Whenever something negative happened or some behavior was disliked, it was downplayed or overlooked. "We never argue" was the mantra. Disapproval was unacceptable. It was not forgotten, however, and was added to a smoldering list of unspoken complaints. As the list grew, frustration, anger, and doubt grew with it. When the meltdown threshold was finally reached, the lid blew off and their nuclear anger was easily justified. It culminated in a mushroom-cloud explosion, complete with pouting, yelling, screaming, arguing, blaming, demanding, and threatening. Their method of handling gripes—ignoring them until they couldn't take it anymore and then opening fire on each other with deadly and painful emotional bullets—leading to a crescendo of anger and distance and the building of walls between them. Unfortunately, no plan for resolving those unspoken differences and gripes had ever been put into place. The option of evaluating each other realistically as imperfect human beings was never a consideration, and learning to use healthy relationship skills didn't merit even a fleeting thought.

However, bonding had already taken place, and when the relationship crossed the threshold of pretensions, the honeymoon was over. Complaining and arguing from Uranus prevailed at that time, leading to substantial distance and lack of affection between the couple. Arguing who was right and who was wrong, along with frequent *should*-ing, escalated the intensity of the problems. Maybe their intentions were good. Maybe they were trying to get the other person to shape up, so that the relationship could be as wonderful and perfect as each had thought it *should* be. But arguing from Uranus made things worse. Like most people, neither Paul nor Barbara appreciated being corrected by their partner, as if penalized by being told how they *should* think, feel, or behave. Their irrational arguing did not solve the original problem; it served only to increase the ever-widening distance between them.

Hopefully, you can see how this pattern of anger, frustration, list-building, blowups, and wall-building results in an increase in punishment, distance, and eventually the terminal withdrawal of affection, also known as the "wrath of Uranus." What would you expect, maybe a magical cosmic intervention? In an effort to resolve arguments, unfortunately without the aid of cosmic interventions, Paul and Barbara had resorted to magically reassuring each other that each would change. It was a futile attempt to resolve the ever-increasing arguments and miraculously patch the relationship. "I'll change." Oh yeah? Show us your plan of action. "I don't have a plan; I just will." Do you suppose that all of a sudden there is going to be an extraterrestrial awakening with a spontaneous injection of healthy relationship skills? Hmm...unlikely!

After a while, as the magical reassurances failed, a dread of continuing in a downward spiral developed. Healthy reassurance with real plans to learn and use reasonable relationship skills was nonexistent. Without healthy reassurance that included viable action plans for improvement, the relationship begins to wilt and die. For any chance of success, significant changes will be required. Without the changes, they may stay together, but the disappearance of love and any kind of affection is a foregone conclusion. Love will be smothered as wall-building steadily increases the distance between them. They will be trapped in an increasing quagmire of distance, anger, frustration, a sense of hopelessness and possibly even hatred.

Are you in this cycle? Where in the cycle are you? Can it be fixed? Will the wrath of Uranus trip you up and haunt you forever? You have the option of learning new skills. Of course, there are other options. You can maintain the status quo and your misery, or you can leave and face the pain of breaking the bond. But it usually seems to make more sense to at least try working at improving something in which you have made such a large investment. When you are convinced you have made your best effort but then conclude that the relationship is unfixable, then it may be easier to consider leaving. Making a reasonable attempt might be better than leaving and wishing you had at least made an effort. And if it really turns out to be a dead-end relationship, it may still offer you a place to practice your skills. Maybe honing your skills there will make it possible for you to apply them to your next relationship.

How Can I Avoid the Wrath of Uranus?

Two people meet. They are attracted to each other. They begin to get to know each other slowly over time. They have good self-acceptance, and even though they each may think the other is generally a terrific person, they maintain healthy skepticism. This allows them to accept that each is a flawed and fallible human being, with pluses and minuses. They can handle discussions about likes and dislikes, and can evaluate their compatibility in a reasonable way. They can scrutinize each other for signs of rigidity: *should, must, have to, got to, need to*. They can evaluate each other's beliefs about healthy relationships, with each taking responsibility for their own thoughts, feelings, behavior, and happiness. They make ongoing attempts to communicate openly, freely, and reasonably. They have an opportunity to offer reassurance in word and deed to each other that they are trying their best to improve the relationship.

Of course, it is always possible that one of the prospective partners may be rejected because one of them does not believe the relationship is in their best interest, and they choose to end it. If they choose to end it, there may be some pain at this point. It is important to note that feeling pain when you leave a relationship does not mean you loved the person. It means that you were bonded to them. You can decide to move on, endure the pain, and go on with your life. Reconsider giving in to advice to go with your heart in this situation, because we have already seen that the limbic system can lead us astray. Whoever gives you that kind of advice obviously doesn't have much of an understanding of neuroanatomy, and if you have forgotten, then go back and reread Chapters 4 ("Where Do Feelings Come From—Mars? Venus? Uranus?") through 6 ("Is It Love, or What?").

If you think there is compatibility and you choose to stay with this person, you can continue getting to know them and continue to bond with them. You can continue to learn their likes and dislikes and can continue to feel closer to them because you are getting to know them, all of their parts, better. You can work on increasing your flexibility, communication skills, showing concern, being considerate and honest, and increasing your enjoyment of the time you spend together. You are forming a partnership based on healthy rules and real closeness. You can focus on positive interactions and increasing behaviors that each person likes. You both can work on decreasing behaviors that the other does not like. When a problem or conflict does arise, each person can take responsibility for their own thoughts, feelings, and behaviors, and their own hurt and happiness. If one person has a concern about the other, they can discuss the problem, provide a reasonable action plan, and give reassurance that they are making their best effort to improve their responsibility and accountability in the relationship.

Healthy Reassurance

Can you see the importance of self-acceptance, flexibility, and self-responsibility? Do you understand how important it is for you to have concern about your partner's feelings even though you do not take responsibility for their feelings? Healthy reassurance is also important. It emphasizes the common goal of having a practical action plan for resolving problems. It is not a magical solution, like "I'll just change," but a reasonable plan of action. It is a practical plan with a goal of decreasing the chance of the problems occurring and recurring, and for dealing with and resolving problems in as timely a manner as possible when they do occur. Having a reasonable action plan is very important when you are giving reassurance; it separates real reassurance from blowing smoke. For instance, compare these two statements: "I am going to make a better effort to call next time I am late" versus "I am writing myself a reminder to call next time I am late." Try to see the benefits of realistic reassurance given in conjunction with a realistic plan. This will allow your relationship to have a much better chance to succeed and flourish. Empty promises eventually wear thin. You and your partner will realize the rewards of your efforts. You will find that making a practical plan when trying to solve concerns is much preferable to blowing smoke with empty promises to change. Empty promises are very common on Uranus. Try at all costs to avoid making them, because not only are they incredibly destructive to a relationship but they also can be embarrassing. Have you ever been accused of blowing smoke? It is a foolproof way to alienate your partner.

CHAPTER EIGHT

The Thrill Is Gone

DO YOU HAVE GOOD relationship skills? Or have you unfortunately been living and breathing the suspect relationship skills from Uranus your entire life? Have you had bad luck picking Mr. or Ms. Right? Does your relationship résumé say, "If it wasn't for bad luck I wouldn't have any luck at all"?

On Uranus they have bad luck in relationships. They think that the relationships just up and spontaneously evaporate without any obvious reason. "It *must* just be bad luck." Is that what you think? Maybe it's always the other person's fault? Perhaps you think you just *need to* find that perfect soul mate. Maybe you just haven't yet found true love. On Uranus everyone expects to have a magical solution to their relationship woes. Look around—most people would love to have an easy magical solution that would make their relationships work. "Love conquers all. I deserve a wonderful relationship. It'll work out because I want it to so bad. I *need* it to work out." Who knows, you might have gotten lucky or you might have gone through many prospective partners and found one that is a good fit. Now what? Did you earn an A+ in Relationships 101, or did you take Auto Mechanics, Woodshop, Swahili, or Basket Weaving instead? Do you feel lucky? Or maybe you just know it will be different this time. "We're so in love."

If we told you there is a high probability that you don't know how to have a healthy relationship, would you believe us? If we told you that more than likely your lack of relationship skills would doom your chances of success for fully participating in a long and happy relationship, would you listen? Many people will go to their grave clinging to primitive magical beliefs about relationships. Believing in magical solutions to relationships is much easier than working to acquire the skills required for enhancing the prospects of a healthy long-term relationship. Are you still waiting for that wonderful magical relationship to fall out of the sky and into your lap?

Do you remember how Barbara and Paul were so in love until they had "had it up to here"? Do you remember how they didn't choose each other while exercising healthy skepticism and how they didn't find out very much about each other's beliefs and behaviors in advance? Well, they also didn't know that the most important part of the relationship is *relating*. Their communication was dismal. Let's be straightforward—it was pretty pathetic. They didn't express their opinions, their specific likes and dislikes, to each other in a healthy way. They did not accept themselves as being flawed and fallible humans, so how could they possibly accept their partner as also being flawed and fallible? They talked to each other with *shoulds* and *musts*. The rigidity of their thinking made compromising and problem solving nearly impossible.

They only admitted they had a problem when catastrophe struck. Do you remember how they failed to take responsibility for their own feelings, their own upset, and their own happiness? They didn't ask for what they wanted. Their logic was this: If their partner really loved them, that partner would know what they wanted. Of course, that kind of magical logic works if your partner is an expert mind reader, but we wouldn't suggest holding your breath for that to happen. Barbara and Paul swept problems under the rug, one that was clearly not a magic carpet. In effect, they were on their own but didn't recognize it.

When they finally did attempt to deal with their incredible backlog of problems, they upset themselves a great deal. They became so angry, and the list of complaints had grown so long, that they frequently didn't even remember why they were so mad. They had been using unhealthy rules from Uranus throughout their relationship. Their gripes and complaints were seldom dealt with in a healthy way. They didn't ask for what they wanted because they believed that their partner *should* know. What a formula for disaster, a guaranteed way to slowly build dislike, dissatisfaction, anger, and even hatred in the relationship. They did everything it took to destroy the relationship while magically believing that their relationship was special and love would keep them together. They assumed that they knew how to have a relationship.

Let's look at some simple solutions that prevent the buildup of anger and despair and that help with keeping relationships at their best and keeping the love alive. Love blossoms from liking someone and interacting with them in a generally enjoyable way. Love doesn't mean never disagreeing with someone or never telling someone you disapprove of some of their behaviors. Traditionally, people in love believe in only accentuating the positive. It is a felony to express any criticism. They don't realize that how they express their disapproval and negative feelings is just as important, if not more important, than only hanging on to or fabricating the positive. Unexpressed and irrationally expressed dislikes are like relationship poison. Each person's dislikes are an important part of them and are just as important as their likes. If the dislikes are not expressed in a healthy way, the other person will never get to know a more complete you, until that fateful day when the *shoulds* hit the fan.

If you are just now looking for or meeting a prospective mate, be sure that you let them know that you think your likes and dislikes are equally important. Let them know that it is important to you to discuss each other's preferences on an ongoing basis and in a reasonable way. However, if you are already in a relationship, then it is equally important that you work on expressing your likes and dislikes in a reasonable and healthy way. Hopefully, your partner will reciprocate. We will discuss fixing your partner in Chapter 11 ("Fixing Your Partner and Others")—while keeping in mind that you will most likely have to work at fixing yourself first. You might be thinking to yourself, "Speaking up to my partner about behaviors that I don't like is like sticking my head in a lion's mouth. How can I offer any criticism without getting my head bitten off?"

Criticizing Your Partner
Hey, this is important: We're talking about healthy criticism...criticism expressed in a *healthy* way. There is a much healthier way to express yourself than pouting or yelling or withdrawing when your partner has done something you don't like. Have you ever heard that old expression: "It's not what you say but how you say it"? "I don't like that" is received much better than "You *shouldn't* do that." It is received much easier because you are expressing your opinion and are talking about the person's behavior rather than judging them as a person.

Opinions are much easier to tolerate than *shoulds*. Expressing yourself with opinions typically works much better than telling your partner what they *should* or *shouldn't* do. You will find that your opinions will be much easier for them to accept if you state your opinion as a preference. Remember, it's only your opinion. It is your preference and not an undisputed and rigid *should* from the sheriff of the universe. Opinions help you to avoid the arguing about right and wrong that frequently accompanies *should* statements. With opinions, you eliminate the desire to rigorously defend your rigid *shoulds*. Again, when you offer criticism, realize that your statement addresses the behavior, not the person. There is a big difference between "I would prefer that you don't do that, because I don't like the behavior" and "I don't like you, you jerk." Again notice the difference between your preferences and labeling: "I am not fond of the behavior; I think the *behavior* is unacceptable" versus "I am not fond of you; I think *you* are unacceptable."

Work hard to avoiding labeling people as other than imperfect human beings. Focus instead on commenting on, critiquing, or praising the behavior and not the person. Try to give your opinion on what they did that you didn't like or what they didn't do that you wanted, rather than labeling them and *should*-ing on them. After all, it is their behavior that you are concerned about. Of course, it is also important to let your partner know behaviors you like, especially if they do something you really like or if it is something that is very important to you. Don't forget that there are many different ways to say something. If you are looking for the best outcomes, be sure to think it through in order to express yourself in a manner that will likely get the best results.

Do you, like many people, have trouble speaking up? This is a very common problem. As children, many of us were taught—or we inferred—that we "should be seen and not heard." Or we were punished in some way for speaking up. Few people that we know were applauded when they jumped up at the dinner table and criticized their parents. To be sure, it is rare to find anyone who grew up being taught to express their opinions, including criticism, in healthy ways. It is no wonder that the tradition of not speaking up when you first meet someone evolved. And it is certainly understandable why speaking up is rare in intimate relationships. It is no wonder, then, that having the skills to speak up and being able to voice your opinion in a reasonable way are rare indeed. Practice using that voice of yours, even if you feel uncomfortable, and learn to bring up your dislikes as well as your likes. However, also diligently work on expressing your preferences in the most reasonable way. In other words, the number one recommendation is to take time to think before you speak whenever possible.

The 48-Hour Rule
It is important not to let your grievances build over time. When you don't speak up and air your grievances, they tend to accumulate. On Uranus, anger and resentment fester and boil for days, months, years, decades, and beyond. This anger is evidenced only by intermittent eruptions of fiery sarcasm, punishment, distance, and withdrawal of affection. Such a noxious smoldering mix is most definitely a real love killer! Here is a handy little trick that tends to prevent negative buildup of these relationship toxins: the 48-Hour Complaint Rule.

The rule will help you practice expressing your concerns as soon and as reasonably as possible. Let's assume that 48 hours is usually enough time to allow you to think about your grievance or complaint, and to think about a way to express it in the best and healthiest manner. You and your partner agree to bring up any and all complaints within 48 hours of whatever event it is that you want to complain about. In effect, this allows problems to be addressed as they come up. It also allows for some cooling-off time so that you can think things through rather than irrationally addressing your concerns by impulsively reacting in an impromptu moment of anger. You may not always solve the problem within the 48 hours, but at least you will have more than likely thwarted an unhealthy buildup of toxic complaints.

A very important part of the 48-Hour Complaint Rule is that if you do not bring a complaint up within the 48 hours, it is unfair to bring it up later. If you do not bring it up within 48 hours, you are forbidden, forever and ever and ever, and then some, to ever mention it. Unless you have a waiver, you have chosen to not express that particular dislike and to move on. Hopefully, you have reasonably concluded that the dislike is not such a big deal because the relationship thrives on both partners expressing their concerns. By the way, once the complaint is lodged, it can be brought up again in a reasonable way. You may then discuss the issue again at a later time as you deem fitting and of course in a rational, healthy, and reasonable manner, as pleasantly as possible.

Attempt to resolve the issues by either agreeing to make changes or accepting behaviors as they are expressed, if tolerable. You may decide to put your concerns on the back burner for later discussion. Of course, you know by now that most of this is negotiable, so this will give you a great chance to practice your negotiating skills. But what if something comes up that you think is a serious deal-breaker?

Sorting Things Out
There may be many dislikes or issues that you prefer would not occur in your intimate relationships. These may include issues such as indiscretions and "fooling around," manners, *shoulds*, and name-calling or labeling. You'll notice that some dislikes you feel very strongly about, some don't seem so important, and some may be deal-breakers. It is best if you can distinguish the level of importance of that concern for you. You may be willing to forget about it and blow it off. Rather than being mistaken, bring it up if you're in doubt. If not, forget it...let it go and move on. On Uranus, people pretend to ignore dreadful behaviors and then upset themselves about them for eternity.

Buckets

If you want to have the benefits of intimacy with your partner, it is important to at least have the choice to bring up and discuss any concerns that you have on as frequent a basis as agreed. And it is vital that you make a great effort to remember and express the positives. It's also a good strategy for each of the partners to think things through on their own in order to be able to clarify their likes and dislikes. Think of it as having three buckets, labeled *likes, unimportant,* and *dislikes.* You can rate and prioritize each item on your own scale with intensity from minimal to maximal, using whatever terms you like, such as *mild, moderate, strong, very strong,* and *nuclear catastrophe.* Take time to prioritize your concerns. Some priorities may change over time, and some may apply only in certain situations. The importance lies in letting your partner know. Think about your concerns carefully and try to be as accurate as possible. It is important that both partners to be up front with their priorities. It is especially important to identify the potential *dealbreakers,* the behaviors that you feel would make your long-term participation in the relationship untenable. It's a good idea to write all of these down. You will be adding much clarity to the relationship.

If you are not currently in a relationship and are looking around, knowing your priorities will help you clarify the "real you" for potential new partners. While you are doing this exercise, you will find it also very helpful to work on identifying and clarifying not only which things you dislike but also which ones you like—your preferences. Then you can sort your relationship opinions into those three buckets, focusing on priorities and intensity.

You can sort your dislikes into the following buckets:

Bucket 1: items that are not a big deal and that you are willing to ignore

Bucket 2: items very important to you that are somewhat negotiable
Bucket 3: Items that you consider potential deal-breakers

You can sort your likes into these buckets:

Bucket 1: items that you would like to have but can live without
Bucket 2: items that you feel are very important to have but are somewhat negotiable
Bucket 3: items that you feel strongly about and that are potential deal-breakers if absent

Here are two ways to bring up dislikes in a generally pleasant manner that will usually get your partner to listen to them, or at least improve the odds that your partner will consider them:

"I would *prefer* you didn't do that" rather than "You *shouldn't* do that."
"I really don't like it when you do that" rather than "You *shouldn't* be that way."

Hopefully, you will use preferential statements such as "I want," "I wish," "I prefer," "I would rather," and "I think it would be better if." By all means, avoid labeling the person: "You jerk," "You worm," "You skunk," or "Hey, stupid." Avoid words and phrases that rigidly demand, such as *should, must, have to*, and *need to*. Work at making "I" statements rather than "you" statements. This tactic at least increases the chances of problems being addressed as they arise, rather than leaving them to fester for eternity, ultimately becoming malignant and leading to a relationship disaster.

Be careful of the "if you really loved me" statements. You know the ones. Sometimes you actually say them out loud. Sometimes you only think it or infer them. "If she really loved me, she would know. If he really loved me, I wouldn't *have to* ask or remind him or tell him twice." About all you will do with this approach is needlessly upset yourself and question your status with the other person. After all, this faulty logic suggests, "If they loved me, they would do it. Since they didn't do it, they *must* not love me. Maybe I'm not lovable." You're still just guessing, so don't make it a love issue. Healthy thinking and good communication will do more to improve a relationship than will magical thinking, wishing and hoping, or believing in the tooth fairy.

If Paul and Barbara had communicated better about their gripes as they occurred, had been more straightforward about likes and dislikes, and had reinforced the positives, they would have greatly improved their chance for relationship success. Their problems could have been resolved as they went rather than left to pile up and fester into hatred and anger, and they might have avoided the Big Bang.

The Rut
We've pointed out the importance of identifying and expressing your dislikes. Don't ignore the importance of also telling your partner what you like. Barbara and Paul unwittingly fell into a rut of taking each other for granted. This is not uncommon in humans because we tend to discount what we expect. When expectations are met, we write them off without credit. But when they don't occur, we impose a penalty. Barbara and Paul fell into a rut and stopped telling each other how much they liked the passion, the hugs, and the kisses: "Sweetheart, I really like it when you do that!" They forgot the approach that had gotten them what they wanted early on in the relationship. They slowly fell into complacency and took each other for granted as they began to draw apart. Believe it or not, some people like taking things for granted because it seems so simple and effortless.

But Barbara and Paul also forgot about the benefits of positive reinforcement, which usually works better than punishment and ignoring.

Polite and affectionate requests beats the stuffing out of the "You *should* do it" approach from Uranus. The demanding approach of stooping to *shoulds* comes across as parental, which over the long run tends to destroy healthy interaction. Work hard not to fall into complacency because you think, "They're *supposed* to," "I *deserve* it," "They *owe* it to me," "If they really loved me," or "It just takes too much effort." These are great strategies to drain the air out of a relationship. Try to be first to acknowledge and reinforce the good stuff, the things you like. Let your partner know what you want in a reasonable way and ever so kindly let them know that you appreciate it when you get it.

Punishment Prevails

Unfortunately, on Uranus most people have learned to punish behaviors that they don't like. They lack skills for reinforcing behaviors in healthy and reasonable ways, the skills that actually tend to get a person more of what they say they want. This is probably a habit learned a long time ago from adults in their life. Children are frequently punished if they make a mistake, while their good behaviors and accomplishments are all too often ignored, taken for granted, or deemed not good enough. Parents are frequently much better at doling out punishments than rewards. If you have the tendency to punish, then make an extraordinary effort to positively reinforce the behaviors you like and want in your partner.

Try to avoid fearfulness and to ask for things you prefer. Hopefully, you are encouraged to speak up about your preferences and you are willing to practice saying things such as "I love it when you do that," "That was really nice of you," "That is such a turn-on," and "I really appreciate it when...." Try not to overlook the benefits of saying *please* and *thank you*. Often, when *please* and *thank you* begin to disappear in a relationship, it is a sign of pending complacency, taking the relationship for granted—the proverbial rut. Try to work on increasing the positive reinforcement; at least you won't sound like a critical, demanding parent. And it is much more likely that in the future, the reasonable partner you picked will repeat the behavior you preferred and will reward it. When you both are working to improve the relationship by discussing the negatives and accentuating the positives, you are on your way to bilateral mutual double-positive reinforcement. Please do not take things for granted that can deflate most any relationship.

Do you still wonder why the thrill is gone? Do you see how you may have contributed to extinguishing it, intentionally or not? Well, maybe the thrill is not gone. Or if it is gone, you might consider working to try to get it back. It might take significant effort from both you and your partner to successfully regain it. It may not turn out to be *exactly* the same as it was early on, but chances are it will be a big improvement. Be willing to work hard to get the relationship that you want, and hopefully the thrill, or a reasonable facsimile, will be there for a long time to come. Take responsibility for your own happiness and the success of your relationship, and for keeping alive the passion and excitement. Work hard at owning up to that responsibility.

CHAPTER NINE

Fine-Tuning Your Relationship Skills

COOPERATION, COMPROMISE, AND GOOD communication are essential ingredients for fine-tuning your relationship. Identifying and clarifying your own preferences and opinions, and getting to know those of your partner, are a very important part of achieving closeness. Communication allows real intimacy by helping you to get to know the real person, and lays the groundwork for cooperation and compromise. Verbal communication is likely the most effective mode of expression for conveying your likes and dislikes. The accuracy and clarity of the verbal communication is very important because it helps minimize misunderstandings and allows your partner to know your perspective on an ongoing basis.

Body Language
Besides verbal communication, body language is frequently an important aspect of communication. Body language includes postures, gestures, and facial expressions. For instance, an upright posture and steady eye contact suggest that you are interested and invested in what your partner is saying. These

behaviors communicate that you care about their opinions, whereas slouching and not maintaining eye contact can imply disinterest and boredom, whether intended or not. Small adjustments in how you communicate with your body, as well as with words, can substantially influence the tone and possible outcome of your conversations. Also, your choice of words, voice tone, and inflection influence the effectiveness of your communication. In a sense, silence is a form of communication, but a form that is usually hard to interpret. The most accurate way of communicating what is going on with you is telling your partner. Otherwise, it is only a guess. It may be an educated guess, and it may even occasionally be correct, but it is still a just a guess and the equivalent of mind reading.

Mind Reading

Mind reading is probably the worst form of communication. It has little use in healthy relationships. Because of the ambiguity involved, it usually creates more problems than it solves. For example, your partner avoids directly communicating to you yet expects you to indirectly know what is on their mind: "You *should* know, and if you really loved me, you would know." Sometimes you might make a lucky guess or an educated guess that is on the money. Typically, this will increase faulty assumptions and lead to noncommunication and even more guessing in the future. You may decide that there's no use in talking to them. You think, "I already know what the answer is going to be." Well, you really don't. You just think you do.

Imagine the poor couple from Uranus in which each partner continually expects the other partner to know what is on their mind or what they want:

"I *shouldn't* have to ask."
"They *should* know."

FINE-TUNING YOUR RELATIONSHIP SKILLS 107

"They *should* want to do it out of love [or respect or common sense]."

"If I *have to* ask, it isn't worth it. It's not the same, and it takes away the value."

In the meantime, the partner doesn't know and really can't figure out why the other person is grumpy, moody, depressed, or something else entirely. Then the unhappy partner has had enough and unloads on their unsuspecting mate and says what's really on their mind. "Why didn't you tell me," the unsuspecting partner asks. The unhappy partner then responds with the assumption "You *should* have known." Is that incredibly ridiculous thinking from Uranus, or what? It is certainly a lousy substitute for reasonable, straightforward, explicit communication.

Mind reading is a very toxic habit, especially when used in the heat of an argument and especially when you use it to overly upset yourself. Granted, this seems like an important time to express your opinions. However, mind reading when you are overly emotional further distorts any attempt to understand and resolve issues with any degree of reasonability. Mind reading makes it almost impossible to settle an issue that is important to you. Even though we might recognize signs of distress or pleasure in a tone of voice, gestures, or facial expressions, they are crude tools for resolving conflict. Accurate communication is preferable to guessing and assuming.

Engaging in Advanced Telepathy
If you do catch yourself frequently mind reading, you are probably guilty of grossly distorting reality. If you are doing a lot of mind reading or requiring it of your partner, it raises suspicions about your motives. You are insisting on defying the reasonable rules of communication. What is on your hidden agenda? Are you expecting telepathy from Uranus? Are you afraid to

speak up? Are you afraid to ask your partner to speak up? Are you afraid of how your partner will respond? Do you fear their wrath, laughter, or an old-fashioned no? Do you rate yourself as a partner by your mind-reading ability? Perhaps you believe that good partners *should* just spontaneously know what is going on in the mind of their partner, and that such a capability proves love, compassion, interest, and empathy. Do you also believe that pigs can fly, that the Earth is actually flat, and that if you just keep digging you'll end up in China? (Please do not try that last one; the Earth's core is made of molten magma, and you will be burned to a crisp before you even get close.) We sincerely hope that you know better, so let's fly back to a not-so-mystical place called reality. Trying to pawn off assumptions and mind reading as thinking suggests that you are taking your cues from Uranus and are capable of being easily duped into believing such silly nonsense.

Mind reading usually only makes things worse in the long run. There are some mind readers from Uranus who are so skilled in telepathy that they can have an argument with another person in which they can actually carry on both sides of the argument, hardly letting the other person get a word in edgewise. That is pretty impressive. Maybe you know them? Hopefully it's not you. Please don't let mind reading suck the breath out of your communication and wreak havoc on your relationship.

Improving Your Odds
You can consider taking a risk and playing the odds. Ask your partner what they are thinking and what is going on with them. Hopefully, they will tell you. You will find that asking, rather than mind reading, helps increase the accuracy of communication. Of course, they may sometimes say, "Nothing," but they say it in a manner in which you suspect that there is something wrong. Then what do you do? What do you do when you suspect

that "nothing" means "something"? Here is a suggestion for how to handle it:

> You approach your partner, keeping your body language in mind, and you actively project your interest and concern. "What's the matter, honey?"
>
> Your partner, on the other hand, is slouching slightly; their hands may be in their pockets, eyes downcast. "Nothing!" they answer, their tone telling you a different story. Maybe it sounds too sharp, dejected, quiet, or dismissive.
>
> So you try again, reaching out to touch their arm in a gesture of concern and comfort. "Are you sure?"
>
> "Yep!" they reply, perhaps shrugging your hand off and looking away. Remember this body language and what it projects. Those memories will be handy when you are on the receiving end of things and trying to remain calm and reasonable.
>
> "Well, if there is anything you want to talk about, I'll be in the living room."

You can then go entertain yourself in the living room or wherever, rather than continuing to pester your partner. If you keep asking, it may appear that you are trying to aggravate the situation. The space you give them after this attempt at communication may allow your partner to think about a better way to handle things. If you pressure them, they might lean a bit, but they do not *have to* talk to you and will get a lot of attention as you seek to extract some intelligent conversation. You might inadvertently reinforce poor communication with your partner. But if you give them some space, then later after the situation has passed, you can discuss your preference that they share a little more information the next time you perceive something is out of kilter. See if you can get some suggestions from them on how they would like you to handle the situation in the future.

This works both ways. Most people occasionally become stressed, upset, or concerned about something. Giving your partner suggestions about how you would like things handled when you are feeling this way may be helpful in future situations.

Sometimes mind readers will hold back for fear of getting a dreaded no. Look on this as a great opportunity for you and your partner. Give them the chance to tell you no. Sure, you might not like it, but show them that both you and the relationship can handle a no. Fight the belief from Uranus that "I *must* never say no or it will offend my partner, they will get angry, or they will dislike me and leave me. Therefore, I *must* tell them yes and always appease them and never disagree." Think, consider speaking up, and try to avoid depriving others of the opportunity to tell you no.

Remember, mind reading is a primitive habit from Uranus. Human brains, similar to the brains of other mammals and nonhuman primates, normally display sensitivity to certain behaviors of others in their environment. This is not a substitute for accurate communication. You probably learned to believe in exploiting mind reading at an early age. It may have become a habit. Maybe this was the way your family allegedly communicated, or how it worked in your early dating relationships. Begin to work on breaking the habit today. Think about and practice speaking up about your opinions, and don't forget to verbalize their intensity rather than reacting emotionally. This allows your partner to get the real picture of how important each opinion is to you. Of course, it will help if you look in your buckets that you filled in Chapter 8 ("The Thrill Is Gone"), but it still requires putting things in the present context.

Heated Arguing Versus Discussing

Let's assume that you have set the goal to have a responsible, reasonable, healthy, and positive relationship by using good communication skills. Hopefully, your partner is on the same page. It usually takes great effort from both partners to work out differences of opinion while balancing the ups and downs in a relationship. But even if your partner does not have the same goals, it is still up to you to maintain your efforts and practice improving your skills in order to make healthy choices for yourself. To facilitate achieving your goal of settling differences of opinion as reasonably as possible, it is important that you try to discuss cooperatively rather than argue competitively about who is right and who is wrong. What is the difference between a discussion and an argument? In a discussion you will hear many "I" statements; in an argument you will hear many "you" statements. There is a long history of feeling wronged behind an argument. The criteria for reasonable discussions are related to the rules of critical thinking. Critical thinking implies the use of certain rules for sound reasoning useful for civil discussions. There are a few books on this topic in Appendix III ("Recommended Reading") if you are interested in further exploration. Yes, the skill could have a better, less intimidating name than "*critical* thinking," but try not to let that scare you off.

Accusations, Fault, and Blame

There are signals that might tip you off that a discussion is turning into an argument from Uranus. There frequently will be statements beginning with the word *you*, along with accusations and blaming. "It is *your* fault." "*You* caused it." Such "you" statements indicate that one person is focused more on the other person's behavior rather than their own behavior. It is equivalent to pointing a finger. "You" statements are usually used to direct blame at the partner. This is almost guaranteed to lead to and escalate an argument. "You" statements frequently contain *should*-isms:

"You *shouldn't* have done that [*or* said that *or* thought that *or* even have thought about thinking that]."

"You *shouldn't* have felt that way."

"You *should* have done it this way," which usually means "You *should* have done it *my* way. Of course this is the right way, since I have nominated myself the keeper of the rules of the universe, and woe be unto those who break them."

From here, the disagreement usually continues to expand and evolves into a full-blown pissing contest not just about "You are wrong and I am right" but instead about who is the bad guy and who is the good guy. "You are wrong and I am right. Unless you admit that you are wrong and I am right, and admit that I am superior, more wonderful, and the conqueror of all, then I *must* use every irrational trick in the book to prove my superior thinking." So be careful and don't forget that these are only your opinions. You might ask, "How can I bring up my own complaints about the other person without using the word *you*?"

"I" Versus "You"

"I" statements offer a great advantage over *you* statements. Practice making "I" statements; focus on the *behavior* that concerns you: "I don't like it when you behave in that way." Remember to label the behavior rather than the person, and by all means express your concerns preferentially, as your opinions. "I" statements focus on your opinions and avoid blaming and finger-pointing, which usually only lead to escalating the argument and causing further deterioration in the relationship. And refrain from trying to make more of it than it is—just an opinion—by using an overgeneralization: "You *always* think that way [*or* feel that way *or* act that way]."

Black Versus White Versus Gray
Overgeneralizations are black-and-white statements that overstate the point, stretching the facts. If you *have to* stoop to using generalizations in the course of your discussion, you might just be better off clamming up until you can express yourself more rationally. Watch out for statements that include *always, never,* and *everyone knows.* They are overgeneralizations and quite unhealthy indicators that the person is trying to prove a point from Uranus. Logically, you can appreciate that *always* and *never* are really pretty rare. And rationally, everyone doesn't know it if you don't know it. Even if you know it too, it is highly unlikely that everyone knows or agrees with any given statement. Be suspicious if you or anyone else is using overgeneralizations to try to prove a point. If someone has to enlist that kind of subterfuge to make a point, it is a very good indication that there is a serious lack of credible evidence to support their case. It reeks of the irrational. When you use informed opinions to get your point across, you are rarely tempted to stoop to leveraging with overgeneralizations because, after all, it's just an opinion. Of course, old habits are hard to break. Have you ever noticed how just as soon as you say *always* or *never* others almost immediately think of an exception? It kind of looks like overgeneralizations are a pretty desperate strategy. What do you think?

Correct your own overgeneralizations if you notice them or if someone else points them out to you. Reconsider your statement and try to eliminate your faulty thinking. And if you are on the receiving end, try to point out the folly of overgeneralizations in a relatively gingerly manner. Help the other person out by volunteering that maybe they really meant to use *often, most of the time,* or *sometimes.* Be warned, however, that in the heat of an argument your partner may not thank you for pointing out their irrational statements.

Here are some tips on how to have a discussion rather than an argument:

- **Avoid blaming.** Use "I" statements instead of "you" statements.
- **Avoid arguing absolute right or wrong.** These are only your opinions. In some cases there even may be a general consensus of right and/or wrong involved, but there is no law that says it is a black-and-white issue. And even if it looks like right or wrong, reducing issues to opinions makes them much easier to discuss.
- **Avoid rigidity.** Avoid using *should, must, have to, got to, need to,* or *ought to.*
- **Avoid rating and labeling a person.** Focus on the behavior instead.
- **Avoid *always*, *never*, and *everyone knows*.** These are overgeneralizations that are usually inaccurate and highly unlikely to be helpful. The statement "You are never on time" is nutty. Even by accident, most every person probably has been on time at least once in life.
- **Avoid saying, "I can't stand it."** You *can* stand it. You have "stood" everything that has ever happened to you in your life. You may not like it, but typically you can stand it.
- **Avoid exaggerating with *awful, terrible,* and *horrible*.** Awfulizing only makes you more agitated, anxious, and upset. Also, doing this makes you not much fun to be around. It is very difficult to talk to someone if they constantly blow things out of proportion. Something may be lousy, annoying, or inconvenient enough without you making it worse by awfulizing. These are usually only magnifications and distortions used to embellish a point. You keep inflating the balloon in an effort to shove aside the other person's opinion or argument, but keep in mind that balloons eventually

deflate and can be popped, especially when you try to stretch them beyond capacity. You might just end up popping the balloon yourself.
- **Take responsibility for your thoughts.** What did I tell myself to upset myself? What feelings did I cause myself to feel that I don't like? What unreasonable thing did I do or say that I really don't want to do or say in the future? How can I work to improve?
- **Try to apologize for any deviations from healthy thinking or behaving that you may have engaged in.**
- **Try to make yourself use "I" statements.** Say, "*I* will try to not upset myself needlessly" or "*I* don't like it when you say that." Use "I" statements to express your opinions and your preferences. Remember, everyone else does not necessarily agree with you, especially if there is criticism involved.
- **Express your dislikes in a healthy way without blaming or threatening.** Replace distortions by addressing behaviors directly and not labeling or rating the person.
- **Accept that you are discussing your likes and dislikes.** You are discussing your opinions, not immutable facts.
- **Accept that everyone has opinions.** You do not *have to* justify them or validate them. It really doesn't matter why you have those opinions, even though it's not a bad idea to occasionally evaluate them for reasonableness. Most everyone can and does have individual opinions, some we agree with and some we disagree with. That is a fact of life.
- **If you feel you may have erred, avoid the tendency to try to justify, signify, dignify, make excuses, or explain your way out of it.** Apologize, apologize, apologize, apologize, apologize, apologize, apologize, and then apologize again. And if in doubt, apologize! If you find yourself

unable to apologize, it is quite possible that you may have apology sensitivity syndrome (ASS). This may require professional intervention. Do you know where it evolved from? Hint: it's a planet.

- **When you are working on a healthy relationship and you make a mistake, consider offering your partner reassurance with a reasonable plan that demonstrates your best intentions to make healthy changes.**

Make a Chart

One way to open your eyes to how often you argue instead of discussing is to make a chart. In one column, enter examples of how you have promoted arguments by using language from Uranus. In a second column, list ways in which you can correct these items in terms of stating preferences, expressing likes and dislikes, avoiding labeling, avoiding overgeneralizations, and so on. Focus on your contribution of unhealthy thoughts and behaviors during prior arguments. Address past instances of differences of opinions that have turned into arguments and where you see that you can make positive changes. You can also address better ways of expressing your concerns about things your partner does that you don't like, things that you would rather your partner do or not do, or other topics of interest. In a third column, write down and ponder examples of how you have corrected unreasonable statements that you have made in the past. Consider how you are now able to replace them with more reasonable examples of healthy communication. This exercise will help you to focus on your responsibility and will help your partner focus on their responsibility in solving disagreements. Hopefully both partners will participate.

Don't forget that it is okay to disagree. Disagreements are a common component of relationships. They can usually be resolved more efficiently by discussion rather than argument. By using more reasonable reference points—that is, healthy rules—your differences of opinions will be less threatening and easier to resolve. Understand that usually most disagreements can be handled in a much more reasonable manner by both parties than you both might think at first. Enlist your partner to work with you toward that goal of increasing healthy communication.

Don't forget that you are trying to overcome some unhealthy habits from Uranus that may have been with you for a very long time. Performing the exercises will help you and your partner to maximize your conflict-resolution skills as best as you can. This strategy will lead to getting more enjoyment out of your relationship as well as out of your individual lives. You also will be showing your partner that you are committed to improving interactions in the relationship. Changing the way you think, the way you process information, is not always easy. It may take a lot of motivation, great effort, and much practice to maximize your success. The concepts are simple, but replacing old habits is not so easy. You are wrestling with one of the strongest forces in the universe, the force of habit. It is a strong force, and you may have to exert a lot of effort to displace it. You'll notice there's a difference between simple and easy!

Here is a helpful tool, called Identify, Challenge, and Replace, to assist you in making changes. (Also see Exercise 5-2, "Changing Unhealthy Thinking," in Appendix II, "Exercises").

1 **Identify** unhealthy thoughts and behaviors.
2 **Challenge** the unhealthy thoughts and behaviors.
3 **Replace** them with healthier options.

With practice, you can make healthier choices for thoughts and behaviors in the future. But without practice, you are much more likely to continue being reactive to your partner and to the world. You will more than likely keep doing the same old thing and keep getting the same old results.

When you do the Identify, Challenge, and Replace exercise, you are focusing on your own individual responsibility for your thoughts, feelings, and behaviors. There is no blaming and no arguing who is the good guy and who is the bad guy or who is right or wrong. Your partner may influence your thinking, feeling, and behaving, but you have the final say. No one made you think, feel, or behave in a certain way. No one can make you act like a bully, jerk, or doormat. You and only you can make that happen. That's good, by the way. It means that you can change how you think, feel, and act. Some old habits die slowly, so get on it right away. But remember that you're not perfect and that from time to time old habits will pop up again, so suck it up again. Fight them down again. Practice, practice, practice!

The exercises provided in this book are designed to help you see the results you achieve in a concrete manner, to help motivate you to keep working, and to provide encouragement. When you experience and record your improvements, it can help you to recognize what works best and fine-tune your communication with your partner. You can look back and turn to what you've written down as you go. (We suggest doing this particularly on those days when it just feels like too much work.) So use your notes. Dieters who keep journals of their progress and goals have a much higher chance at achieving success at not only losing weight but also at keeping it off. So think of these exercises as your relationship diet journal, a way to stay away from and rid yourself of those unhealthy relationship habits. Keep at it! You are on your way to fine-tuning your relationship skills.

CHAPTER TEN

Advanced Training

OCCASIONALLY, A PARTNER IN a relationship makes what they see as a major concession. They do something for the other person that they really don't want to do. They may rather have a root canal than go to a business function, garage sale, movie, or some social event, yet they go anyway, at their partner's request. This is what is known as doing something for "the good of the relationship," and making this kind of compromise may actually enrich your relationship. Ideally this behavior is reciprocated from time to time so that both partners can see that there is balance in the relationship and that both partners give in on occasion. If you don't think your partner is equally reciprocating, which is a fairly common perception, it is your responsibility to speak up. And yes, it's your responsibility to let it be known what kind of reciprocation you want. An agreeable balance is better than a disagreeable imbalance, but since things are continuously changing, we more than likely will have ample opportunities to make adjustments on the fly. Agreeable balancing usually requires negotiating and adjusting, using good communication skills. Why? Simply because things change.

Try to look at your efforts as volunteering and being in your best interest rather than as giving in. Doing things for the good of the relationship from time to time is in your long-range best interest. If both partners are willing to speak up, negotiate, and compromise, all will likely balance out over time. It is the responsibility of both partners to work toward balancing the relationship as much as possible. It is your choice, and yes, you might be inconvenienced now, but you'll be less inconvenienced over time. Cooperation works both ways, and as long as you are cooperating, you can reasonably encourage your partner to cooperate as well.

It is important that when you comply, you remember that it is your choice. Avoid whining and grumbling about it. Try to maintain your good manners and your sense of humor. Make your most pleasant effort. Look at the long-range picture of how this doesn't happen that often. Since it is in your best interest to do things for the good of the relationship on occasion, agreeing to do the unwanted activity and then turning it into a whinefest would be ill advised. In effect, acting that way puts a price on compromises, meaning that though your partner gains your agreement to compromise, he or she then has to pay a price: your whining. Sure, your behavior might teach your partner not to ask you again to take part in the activity you dislike. But it is likely that your behavior will lead to some resentment that may require further negotiation. Who wants a gift that comes with eternal grumbling? Cooperation is a two-way street.

It is up to you to work on maintaining as reasonable a balance as possible. If you don't think there is generally a reasonable balance, it is your job to assert yourself. Try not to feed yourself any of that garbage that the folks on Uranus feed themselves, such as "If he really loves me, I *shouldn't have to* ask. He *should* know," or "She *should* be thinking of me." No one is likely to think of you as often as you do. Remember, just like you are, your partner is a flawed and fallible human being no matter how wonderful, sweet, kind, and loving they happen to be most of the time. For you to magically expect your partner to know what you want, when you want it, and then to blame them if they don't produce is simply unreasonable.

Complaining about the unfairness and imbalances in the relationship without making an active effort to correct any of the perceived imbalances makes you sound like a victim: "They used me. They owe me. It's not fair." When you have a victim's attitude, several things happen:

- You don't get what you want as often as you might otherwise.
- You upset yourself and make yourself needlessly miserable.
- Your partner won't have a clue why you are so unhappy. You will find yourself frequently humming the refrain "Poor, poor, pitiful me" (sung to the tune of "Row, Row, Row Your Boat"), and the rest of us Uranus expatriates will shake our heads and ridicule you for being so predictably whiny.

Enough with the pity party! You are the one volunteering to continue in the relationship, and you volunteered to cooperate. It is a partnership. In relationships, people use each other. That's what relationships are about. The trick is to work at a reasonable range of behavior so that both partners can enjoy balancing mutual use.

On Uranus, partners don't speak up about what they want and don't want. And they don't speak up about what they like and don't like. We could claim that there are almost an infinite number of reasons, but ultimately none of them are really important, because they freeze communication and will almost surely create ongoing problems in the relationship. This lack of expression and rigidly digging in of your heels on ineffective principles seriously affects the ability of you and your partner to engage in healthy communication in the relationship. So what is more important, those principles or the relationship? You and your partner can decide that for yourselves. Think about it: Is sticking to some principle you made up really more satisfying than having a harmonious relationship? If your partner cannot or will not participate, then it is up to you to decide what you want to do. Leaving the relationship is one option. Trying to read your partner's mind is another. But the healthy thing to do may be to try talking with them and demonstrating the benefits of speaking up.

By speaking up, you are modeling the kind of behavior you want them to practice. Remember to refrain from attempting to read their mind or guess what they want. Sure, it's okay to surprise them occasionally, but there is nothing wrong with asking them what they want, what they would like, or what they think. Balance, though, is the key. It is reasonable to ask your partner for their opinion. You are demonstrating that you are concerned about them. When in doubt, ask. Asking doesn't mean that you can't make a move without their opinion. But it does make it obvious that you care what they think. Partners who are not very expressive can learn from your modeling and encouragement. It is up to you to try to be liberal with both of those items.

Getting More of What You Want From Your Partner

Here is a simple, helpful exercise to help you get more of what you want from you partner. Make a list of up to five things that you would like your partner to do, in order of importance. Also note how often you would like for each item to occur: once a week, monthly, every other appearance of Halley's comet? Your list may include requests such as a kiss once a day or breakfast in bed once a week. Ha, ha! Yeah, right! Hey, you never know unless you ask. You can expand your list later. Ask your partner to make a list also. Partners then exchange lists.

These are the rules:

1 **Each partner gets to choose what they are willing or not willing to do.**

2 **Make your request in advance.** Your giving them the list doesn't mean that they will necessarily always remember to perform or that they have nothing else to think about except your list. Don't complain about having to remind them. (We put this rule in for you, guys.)
3 **Be content if and when your partner does something from the list, even if it is not as often as you originally requested.** *Sometimes* is still more frequent than *never* or *rarely*. Focus on what was agreeable to both parties.
4 **Be polite when making your request.** Say *please* and *thank you* to receive bonus points.

Remember that positive reinforcement helps. Sweet nothings and pet names such as *honey* or *sugar* are fine. They are certainly better than *jerk, butthead,* or *dingbat*. Letting your partner know what you *do* want helps. Too often we make the mistake of telling people only what we *don't* want. Yes, it may feel awkward at first. So what? Practicing a new behavior of any sort usually feels awkward! That's normal. That's why you are practicing, to make it more automatic so it feels okay. It will begin to feel normal after a while; just keep practicing. You are looking at a good payoff as you increase your skills. You may just find that you get more of what you want, and that's hardly something to complain about.

Remember, don't be afraid to ask. There was once a woman from Uranus who was told she could probably get more of the things that she wanted if she would only ask for them. She sniffed and stubbornly replied, "I'm not asking. It's not the same if I *have to* ask." She steadily held onto this belief and rigidly refused to change it. One spring afternoon while the woman was out to lunch with some friends, one of the ladies began gushing over the wonderful relationship another of their friends had with her husband. One of the ladies smiled, sighing that she was absolutely green with envy. The woman smiled at the gossip, seeming to dismiss it from her mind a second later. But the discussion stuck with her, as if it took root in the back of her mind. As the seed from the story about her friend's wonderful marriage grew, so did her envy and bitterness over her own less-than-lovely relationship. She soon found it difficult to think about anything else. She continued to torture herself daily about how she seldom got the things that she really wanted from her own relationship, even though she wished and hoped intensely. She heard through the grapevine that her friend's husband almost daily brought home flowers or candy, cards or presents. He even frequently took his wife out to dinner. Their relationship seemed to be everything she kept wishing hers would become. Her friend's husband appeared to be very attentive, the perfect husband.

After several gut-wrenching years, the woman finally approached the friend who had the devoted husband and told her how envious she was of her relationship. When her friend asked what she meant by that, she explained how she had observed all the attentive behavior her friend received from her husband. The friend chuckled and replied, "Oh no, you don't understand. It's not at all the fairy tale you think it is. I *have to* ask him every day to bring me flowers or cards. I *have to* remind him almost every time we're out in public to be affectionate toward me. Believe me, he would be a very forgetful 'prince' if I didn't remind him that I appreciate being treated like a 'princess' now and again." Then the woman from Uranus finally realized that if she only asked, then she might possibly have the same benefits in her relationship. No, having to ask is not the same as getting what you want without asking. She acknowledged, however, after getting some good results, that getting what she wanted by asking was one hell of a good substitute.

Simply put, asking works. It even works better than closing your eyes, crossing your fingers, and clicking your heels together. As gurus around the world have said, "Nothing ventured, nothing gained." Fight the self-defeating belief from Uranus that you *shouldn't have to* ask and that they *should* know. Thinking that you *should* never *have to* ask more than once or never *have to* remind is equally self-defeating. "If they really loved me and cared for me, it would be important enough to them that they would know and remember. And I *should* never *have to* ask twice." Nope, sorry—it's probably not going to happen. Go get a needle and pop that big pink balloon full of crazy gas floating over your head.

Great news: You don't *have to* ask! It just works better than expecting clairvoyance or telepathy. What if we told you that you could get 60 to 90 percent of what you want by asking? Is that better than what you've been getting? Is it better than getting 10 percent or less when you haven't been asking, when you've been resorting to wishing and clicking the heels of your ruby-red slippers together? And if you don't take that gracious offer after asking for it, that points to some unhealthy rules you have developed. Hopefully, rules like that deeply concern you and increase your willingness to make improvements and to consider asking as a reasonable option.

How to Get Less of What You Don't Want

Now here is an exercise to help you get less of what you don't want from your partner. Make a list of five things that you would rather your partner did not do. Put them in order of preference. These are some examples:

- "I would prefer you not belch at the dinner table."
- "I would prefer you not stand in front of the TV when football is on."
- "I would prefer that you not yell at me."
- "I would prefer that you not leave your socks on the kitchen counter."

You can expand past the five items later, once you get the hang of this. Then have your partner also make a list of five things for you.

These are the rules:

1 **Agree to both ask and remind your partner, if appropriate.** Please, no complaining about reminding.
2 **Remember to state the items as things you don't like or don't prefer.** No yelling, and no *should, must, got to, have to,* or *never.* Also, none of the "I can't stand it when you do that" nonsense. Remember, you *can* stand it. You just don't like it.
3 **Don't forget your manners.** Extra points are given for *please* and *thank you.*
4 **Don't forget to notice attempts to follow your preferences.** Grade on the curve, give partial credit, and remember that no attempt—even an accidental one—is too small to be rewarded.

Do this exercise with your partner until they cry uncle—and then do it once more. Continue to work on eliminating your own beliefs from Uranus. You are learning to negotiate and communicate. It might even lead to conscious cooperation. It might even start to happen accidentally, out of habit. Look, Ma, no hands!

Yes, your partner may not want to play. Perhaps disappointing, but so what? You can still change your thinking and even work to eliminate the behaviors they have told you they don't like. After all, these may be skills that you take with you to the next relationship. Damn! Do you believe this? Skills that might help you get more of what you want and less of what you don't want! Yeah, it sounds too good to be true, like a free lunch. Unfortunately, it takes much more effort than wishing and hoping, but you will find that the rewards are well worth the expense.

Warning! For Experts Only:
Mutual Spontaneous Simultaneous Sucking-Up Contest
The Mutual Spontaneous Simultaneous Sucking-Up Contest is a competition to see who can be the nicest and most affectionate partner. This can be a daily, weekly, yearly, or lifetime contest. To participate, each contestant is required to have prior qualification in basic politeness: Please, Thank You, May I, You're Welcome, and Apologizing 101. Additional certification in Advanced Complimenting is recommended but not required. Each contestant tries to display more affectionate behaviors than their opponent. The winner gets to brag about their affection expertise. Both partners agree to specific affectionate behaviors that they would like to see demonstrated more often in the relationship. An arbitrary scoring system is agreed on. Partners then keep track of their scores, and a winner is declared. At bedtime the winner has the opportunity to let the losing contestant add bonus points to even up the score and eliminate any hard feelings. In the event of a tie, there can be a tiebreaker, double tiebreaker, and so on.

Each contestant tries to acquire the most points before they fall asleep and thereby take the lead. The winner is declared the next morning. The loser is then given a head start for the day, an opportunity for them to soar into an early lead. The winner then can make a heroic effort to come from behind for a repeat performance, the elusive double! You will find that a double is very difficult to achieve, and a triple is a rare bird indeed. By the way, even at this level, a contestant may have a bad day. If this occurs, a true champion is encouraged to limit their taunting, maybe even throw in a few freebies, and offer a little support.

Remember, basic politeness is required. Here is list of considerations that you may edit according to your preferences. It begins with a refresher in politeness, complimenting, and sweet nothings. Of course, extra credit is given for complimenting your partner in front of others, and double extra credit is awarded if your mother-in-law is present.

Politeness	"Thank you so much." ~ "I really love it when you do that." ~ "Thank you, thank you, thank you." ~ "I apologize." ~ "Please accept my apology." ~ "Would you please, please, please, please do it just for me?"
Compliments	"You're welcome." ~ "It is my pleasure." ~ "You are so charming." ~ "You are so gorgeous." ~ "I just couldn't help myself." ~ "You are so pretty." ~ "You are so handsome." ~ "You are so cute." ~ "You are so sweet." ~ "You are so nice to me." ~ "You look lovely." ~ "What a lovely thing to say." ~ "You look really sharp." ~ "You are so smart." ~ "I love it when you do that." ~ "I am so lucky." ~ "I really appreciate it when you do that." ~ "You made my day." ~ "You are so affectionate." ~ "You are my favorite girlfriend." ~ "You are my best husband ever." (Hopefully this gets a chuckle . . . but those not still in their first marriage might want to steer clear of this one as a first choice.) ~ "You're welcome." ~ "It is my pleasure." ~ "I just couldn't help myself." ~ "You are so good-looking."
Sweet Nothings	Sweetheart ~ Sweetie pie ~ Sweetness ~ Sugarplum ~ Dear ~ Honey ~ Honeybunch ~ Stud muffin ~ Lover boy/ Lover girl ~ Hunk ~ Babe ~ Gorgeous
Actions	Hugs ~ Kisses ~ Pats ~ Touches ~ Brushes ~ Rubs ~ Holding hands ~ Caresses ~ Loving looks ~ Smiles ~ Fondling (in private only)

Hopefully, at this skill level both partners will display a sense humor and the worst outcome will be a lengthy discussion about who the winner is or a discussion about who is the best partner in the world, and perhaps how each partner can improve their performance with positive reinforcement. Of course, the goal here is to increase positive feelings between partners, so keep that in mind if you decide to discuss improvement. There may even be a double overtime declared to resolve the issue. This is preferable to arguing about who is the worst partner and the biggest whiner in the world! Do unto others as you would have them do unto you, but try to beat them to it. And when it comes to your partner, don't stop there with barely winning—do more for them than you would like for them to do for you. Strive to be the best partner you can be. Hopefully you will realize that this makes you very hard to replace, which is not a bad spot to be in.

Do you want more romance? Some do, and some don't. If you do, then here is the simple solution: Keep displaying the behaviors you were displaying when you were first feeling romantic, when the relationship was new. Of course things were new then, and old is different from new. But if you can continue to get those old behaviors that you liked, it's a pretty good substitute. You may *have to* ask, and you may not get those behaviors all of the time, but who's counting? Of course, avoid letting the toxicity of unresolved issues and conflicts build up. Those are sure romance killers!

Now step back just for a minute and think about all you have learned and accomplished so far. Can you believe it? You are becoming a summa cum laude black-belt relationship master! Keep up the good work, and continually remind yourself of how far you've come since we started! You can even pat yourself on the back if you'd like. You see, flexibility can come in handy.

CHAPTER ELEVEN

Fixing Your Partner and Others

You might have bought this book specifically because of this chapter. It's not unusual for people to focus more on what they perceive as their partner's wrongdoings rather than noticing the error of their own ways. Many people believe that if their partner would just clean up their act, they would have no worries, hassles, or problems, and everything would be wonderful. You might be happy to know that there is a lot you can do to help fix your partner, and it's not all that hard. This chapter takes you through some simple steps, starting with the least disruptive.

**Fix Yourself First,
and Then You Can Work On Your Partner**
We can't stress this enough: You'll have to fix yourself first before you can fix your partner. If you're not able to keep your wits about you, you won't be able to do much for others. A distraught partner typically doesn't do as good a job of relating as a clearheaded partner does. We've talked plenty in this book about blaming another person for your upset. If you still believe that you are

upset only because the other person is misbehaving, maybe you really have made a poor choice of a partner. More likely, you had best go back and read Chapters 1 ("I Love You. You're Perfect. Now Change!") through 4 ("Where Do Feelings Come From—Mars? Venus? Uranus?") again. When you stop thinking from Uranus, dealing with others becomes much easier and can be much more enjoyable. If you are operating out of anger, fear, and upset, you are not as likely to get the results you want.

Model What You Want
Good teachers have known for years that one simple way to get attention and to influence change is to act as the model for the behavior you want from others. It's only fair that you take the lead and behave in a reasonable and healthy manner if you are expecting the same from your partner. "Do as I say and not as I do" sounds parental and hardly encourages cooperation. If you usually deal with your partner in a loud voice, try to use a quieter voice, which is probably a good idea anyway. If you have forgotten the standard rules of politeness, they involve saying *please* and *thank you*. If you don't usually take the initiative to approach your partner for sex or affection, then start doing it, at least on occasion. If you usually pout, cry, scream, whine, wail, or sulk for days on end, consider cutting it out and substituting polite communication.

Set an example and model the behavior that you would like to see in your partner. That doesn't mean you *have to* be agreeable all the time, nor is it realistic for you to expect your partner to be agreeable all the time. It is important how you handle those times when you disagree, as well as how you handle trying to increase the overall positive interaction in the relationship. Remember, your partner is a flawed and fallible human just like you. Accept that as reality. You may do better by gently asserting yourself. You didn't partner up with a mind reader, did you? Even if you believe that you managed to do so, it's still up to you to let them know what you want. It's okay to let them know how hard you are trying to change for the better. But using your "great effort" as weapon to beat them over the head with is hardly recommended. So how can you enlist your partner?

Try to Get Your Partner to Help You Become a Better Partner
Getting your partner to help you become a better partner may sound paradoxical, but it seems to be a pretty effective strategy. You might pick a chapter or theme from this book and tell your partner that you are working on improving your relationship skills. Ask them to help: "Sweetheart, I'm trying to get rid of my nasty *shoulds* and *musts*, but they keep slipping out. Would you please point them out to me? It would be so helpful." The odds are good that your partner will be more than happy to point out your faults—your faulty *shoulds*—but in order to point out your *shoulds*, they will have to know what the hell you're talking about, and this will require paying attention to you when you talk. What an added bonus! This exercise could also help mold them into a better listener. You've just killed two birds with one stone! In order for your partner to better understand what you are asking them to help you with, they may even want to read Chapter 3 ("The *Should*-ectomy . . . Exorcising the *Shoulds* From Uranus"). They just might even accidentally become more aware of their own *should*-ing. You never know—this might even inspire them to read and work through this entire book with you.

Here's a good way to ask: "Dear, I'm trying to take more responsibility for my own feelings. Will you please point it out to me if I try to blame you for my anger, upset, or unhappiness?" The typical response from the partner is "Damn right, I'll help you!" Hey, this is too good to be true. Now look at all the help you're getting.

You could also try this one: "Honey, I'm trying to stop nagging you, and I want to be more positive. Would you mind telling me some things you would like me to do for you? You may have to remind me, but I'm really going to give it my best try." *Bam!* You're given an instant list. Most likely verbal and not written, but that's all right for a starter. Now figure out what, if anything, there is on the list that you are willing do. If there is something that you don't want to do, suggest an alternative. Try not to be too defensive about the list. Just because something is on the list, that does not mean you *have to* do it. Now is probably not the best time to argue over the stuff on the list.

If you have been doing some of the things and yet your partner hasn't noticed, so what? Congratulate yourself and keep trying, and maybe they will notice. Also, remember to do the things on the list again and again and again, even if your partner does not notice. The more you keep doing them, and add in some unexpected variations, the more likely it is that they will notice. If after a dozen times or so they still don't seem to have noticed, ask them about it. Let them know about your great effort, but try not to rub it in. Observe your partner for any new behaviors, even if they didn't ask you what they could do for you. It is not uncommon for others to put forth more effort when they notice their partner making positive changes and they are reaping the benefits. Cooperation is a two-way street, but it does not always *have to* be exactly fifty-fifty.

Egad! Some People May Not Be Willing to Be Fixed
Some people may rigidly refuse to change. They may be so rigid that they are determined to be the winner of the Self-Righteous Partner of the Year contest. They see their way as the only right way, and that's just the way it is. Of course, to make a relationship work in a healthy manner, it normally takes the cooperation and motivation of two people. Only you can decide if the

relationship you're in is worth it. Ask yourself if the relationship is in your best interest. Can you get from it what you want—or most of what you want? Can you remain somewhat happy and relatively mentally intact in spite of not having the ideal relationship you had hoped for? If the answer is a resounding "No way! This plane won't fly, Orville!" then you may decide to bail out and tough it out through the pain and grief of leaving. Breaking the bond and going on your way may be your most viable option, but only you can make that decision.

Hopefully, your partner is interested in making things work better and will cooperate, though don't forget that some partners will not like your changes. They may decide to bail out because you have changed and you are trying to change the rules on them. Even though you may think your changes are for the better, they may not think so. The good news is that you are taking responsibility for your choices and your happiness, and maybe, just maybe, being alone is better than living with the south end of a northbound horse.

Fixing Your Grief
If you decide to leave the relationship, it is possible that you will experience a roller coaster of emotions. At times you might be relieved and overjoyed to be escaping from your partner. At other times, you may waver in your conviction and feel scared to death and ridden with grief. It is not unusual to change your mind and your mood about a zillion times, maybe even in one day. You may feel like a rubber band, stretched to the limit with pain and fear when you pull away, and limp with misery when you come back. A fear of being alone, reluctance to be the bad guy, and concern about the impact of the breakup on others are just a few of the issues that may influence your wavering back and forth. Be prepared, because breaking a bond is painful for most people. Sometimes, even when you have made up your

mind, you might have moments of doubt about your decision. That's typically what happens when someone breaks the bond of a relationship that was once very important. Breaking a bond can be viewed as a grieving process.

Just in case you decide that it's time for you to leave your relationship, here are some tips for rational grieving:

1 Counseling may be helpful.
2 If you become depressed, consider professional help if the symptoms of depression are debilitating or persistent.
3 Focus on you and on taking care of yourself.
4 Be around others, even if you don't feel like it. Friends can be very helpful. Just try not to spend all your time rehashing the relationship and the breakup.
5 Keep yourself busy. Being alone and doing nothing allows you to create doubts by worrying. It allows you too much time with nothing left to do but focus on unwanted negative feelings that can leave you viewing life as a barrel of prune pits.
6 Set aside a special time of day to grieve or just experience your misery. Decide that you will invest 20 to 30 minutes, go into a room, turn off the lights, disconnect the telephone, maybe even sit in the corner, and concentrate on all your misery-producing thoughts. This can help to reduce the intrusion of these thoughts during the day. You are taking charge of your grief rather than letting it taking charge of your life. Instead of letting your grief ruin 24 hours of each day, you are limiting it to 20 to 30 minutes a day. Throughout the rest of the day, work hard to push those negative thoughts away by distracting yourself. Yes, this is easy to say and hard to do. Don't give up. It takes time. Keep working at it, and you will make progress.
7 Work hard not to think about the broken relationship or anything related to it except during the time you have set

aside for grieving. All other times, work at pushing it out of your mind by telling yourself forcefully, "Not now! I will get back to that tonight at 7!" It might be hard to do at first, but do it anyway. Try hard to resist giving up or giving in.

Here are some techniques to help push out the grief and anguish:

- Count backward from 1,000.
- Recite the Gettysburg Address. (Get a copy, carry it with you, and learn it.)
- Do multiplication tables in your head.
- Think about being at the beach with the waves, sand, warm sun, ocean smells, and jabbering seagulls. Watch out for the birds.
- Think of the five senses, and make yourself identify something for each sense. For example, make yourself identify a smell that you can smell right there at that moment. Make yourself identify a taste, right there at that moment. Okay, so you've forgotten what the five senses are: sight, sound, smell, touch, and taste. Now you only have to dig up the Gettysburg Address.

As you steadily do these exercises, you eventually will find that during the time you have set aside for grieving, you are using fewer and fewer boxes of tissues. You will likely find that you are spending less and less time on experiencing guilt-producing anguish, feeling anger at yourself and others, and feeling miserable and depressed. The ability to feel good about the here and now will start to return, and your healthy outlook will slowly break through as you begin to plan your future. This process may be slow for some and quick for others. That is just the way it is. But in time and at your own pace, you can begin to move on and start to make decisions and choices to enhance your happiness, your life, and your future relationships.

When All Else Fails But You Stay in the Relationship Anyway
Sometimes, for whatever reasons, people choose to stay with a particular partner in spite of their self-centeredness and lack of cooperation. If that is the case for you, you can make it your number one goal to reduce your conflicts. Work especially hard on your healthy thinking and behaviors. Sometimes it is helpful to be divorced only in your head. And when things seem their most frustrating, consider the source. You might have given up trying to have a more reasonable and cooperative relationship with someone who is rigid, bullheaded, or difficult to deal with even on a good day. If they did think a little more reasonably about the relationship, it would be different. They don't and refuse to reconsider, so it isn't likely going to change. In the meantime, see what you can do to make yourself happy in spite of what your partner does. Remember that you are responsible for your own happiness and that after all is said and done, it is your choice to stay. It may seem like all of your choices are lousy ones, and staying may not seem like the best choice in the world, but you may feel it's the best thing to do for the time being.

Fixing the Kids

Young Children
As we discussed in Chapter 4 ("Where Do Feelings Come From—Mars? Venus? Uranus?"), children go through an early learning stage when they think in a very concrete, black-and-white manner. Later they develop an ability to think in the abstract. Unfortunately, before they perfect that ability to think, most children endure a barrage of *should, must, have to, need to,* and *got to* from their parents as well as from society. These rules

are typically viewed as immutable. Unfortunately, they circumvent thinking about the consequences of choices. Little regard is given to teaching the importance of making thoughtful choices to get the best outcomes.

When using these *shoulds* and *musts*, the parents are inadvertently sending the message to the children that they do not have choices. This is unhealthy, because the children *do* have choices. However, there are different consequences for different choices. It is much more reasonable to point out the different consequences that can result from specific behaviors than to say, "You *shouldn't* do that." When you as a parent take responsibility for implementing the rules, you also take responsibility for implementing the consequences. It is important that consequences, such as time-outs, be made clear and applied in a consistent and expedient manner. Of course, it would be nice if children would spontaneously behave in the way that parents prefer, but that is somewhat unlikely. So the parents have the option of setting expectations and limits, pointing out the child's choices and consequences, and following through with their role in applying consequences.

Yet it seems that parents frequently use punishments rather than positive reinforcement. More than likely, those parents received more training in punishment than in positive reinforcement from their own parents. Do you see the cycle being perpetuated here? Positive reinforcement is somewhat more sophisticated, requiring more forethought and effort from the parent. Of course, it's much easier to criticize after the fact. It's much easier to tell a kid what they *shouldn't* have done and then whack 'em. With a little more effort, however, parents can generally get better results by using positive reinforcement to increase the behaviors they desire. If a child likes to play computer games but does not like to do homework, the parent can allow the child to earn computer time by completing homework in a timely manner. This reward strategy is usually more effective than punishment. Although it may seem a little awkward at first, the parent will find that it is generally more effective in increasing the desired behaviors. Don't forget to be consistent, or at least as consistent as humanly possible.

Time-out for young children can also work very well for decreasing certain behaviors. During a time-out they are not allowed to have positive reinforcement. Usually this is a better alternative than punishment. When children are raised in this manner, they are more likely to learn the benefits of thinking and of positive reinforcement and to value the consequences of their behaviors. When they learn this thinking strategy in conjunction with effective communication, they also may learn to substitute preferences, may learn to avoid *shoulds* and *musts*, and may be able to view life as a series of choices and outcomes over which they have some control. These are reasonable skills for children to have as they enter adolescence and early adulthood, when they are faced with more independence and responsibility.

Mean what you say and say what you mean. Parents find that they get much better results by being consistent. Consistency makes them more believable. Let children know in clear and concise terms what is expected. Let them know what the rules are and the consequences for their choices. Don't just tell them; help them think it through so that they can at least see how their choices and subsequent consequences are related.

Try to remember that children, like most of the rest of us, want what they want when they want it. Therefore, sometimes they will upset themselves needlessly. They may even throw temper tantrums in public. If a parent gives in to a tantrum, the child will easily learn to leverage this behavior to their advantage and exploit the parent in the future to get what they want. Adults do this too. Although it is an adult version of a temper tantrum, we can see how childlike the behavior is, as if the world revolves around "me, me, me."

Temper tantrums aren't the only behaviors parents can unwittingly reinforce. The older child who cries frequently and is immediately comforted and coddled by the parent may learn an unhealthy way to solve problems. They may be learning a negative way to get hugs and cuddles from parents. It is not unusual for a child to cry and even throw the occasional fit. But these behaviors will generally decrease if left unrewarded by the parent, and they will increase if they work. Stop and think about the various ways parents have accidentally taught kids to continue noxious or unwanted behaviors.

When your child is doing something that you have deemed inappropriate, try to avoid making statements like "We don't do that." It doesn't quite make sense to an observer who is watching the child do it even as you speak. And what is this "we" nonsense? You are the parent and they are the children. There are some rules that apply specifically to them and not to you. It would be more appropriate to point out to the child what the rules are for them, and the consequences for infractions, and then to apply the consequences as appropriate.

Sometimes it is beneficial for parents to stop and review the rules that they use with their children. Why? Because parents often find that they have inadvertently inherited some rules from Uranus that don't make sense. They may have learned these rules during their own childhood. Are the rules reasonable and appropriate today? Were they ever reasonable? Are they reasonable in your situation? Be careful when making a list of ways parents "*should* behave" and the rules they "*should* use" and how children "*should* behave." Even with the best of intentions behind them, rules that preclude choices and consequences for behavior convey an unhealthy way to deal with life's difficulties in the long run.

If the rules have *shoulds*, you can keep the rules, but throw away the *shoulds*. Discuss choices and consequences instead. Make a list of the rules that you use and evaluate them for any remnants of *shoulds*, *musts*, *have to*, and *need to*. Also evaluate the rules for *always* and *never*. You know the drill. After you have done that, go over the list and make reasonable changes. For the *shoulds*, substitute consequences.

When communicating with your children, it is important to express yourself as accurately and precisely as possible. Equally important in raising children is behaving in a reasonable manner toward your partner. You are influencing your children daily as they observe you. The lucky part is that improving your relationship with your partner directly benefits your children. Even if you do not realize it, your children are observing both the way you relate with them and the way you relate with your partner. For them, your behavior to others is the curriculum in Relationships 101 and forms the foundation of the relationship skills, or lack thereof. These are behaviors that they will carry into adulthood.

If you have a child who behaves in unusual ways, don't forget that there may be other things going on, such as a childhood illness. In these instances you may consider an evaluation by a professional. The effects of many childhood illnesses, such as depression and anxiety, can benefit from help by a health-care professional and may require counseling or medication. Attention deficit hyperactivity disorder is an example of a lifelong disorder that begins in childhood, benefits from counseling, and is typically best treated with medication.

Remember, the parents are the adults of the house and have the responsibility of making and enforcing the rules. Try to be as fair as possible, but the rules will not always seem fair to all involved. This mimics the real world, where rules rarely seem fair to everyone. But there is no rule that says that rules *must* be fair. As the parent you can try to make the rules as fair as possible and to apply them in a consistent manner, but the bottom line is that you are responsible for setting, enforcing, and reinforcing the rules.

Adult Children
Try not to rob your adult children of the opportunity to learn from their mistakes; don't always try to save them making errors. There may be some exceptions, but your parental tendency to rescue them is likely reinforcing continued dependence. It also conveys your own lack of belief in the development of their adult ability to take responsibility for making their own choices and learning from the resulting consequences. If you really love them, how could you possibly want to rob them of these valuable learning experiences?

Fixing Others

Parents and Friends
If you want to improve your relationship with others, try to use the same skills that you are learning in order to improve your relationship with your mate.

You may have difficulty relating to your parents. They may barrage you with *shoulds*. They might try to guilt-trip you at every turn, but fear not. Those days are over (almost). You used to think that *they* made you angry or guilty or hurt your feelings. But obviously this is not so. If you still doubt it, go back to the beginning of the book and keep rereading until it sinks in. If that's what it takes for you, try not to be overly concerned to the point of worrying, because repeating and practicing is normal. It can take a few times, especially when you're approaching your godlike—or possibly Godzilla-like—parents, at least to your mind.

You are responsible for your feelings, the good ones, the bad ones, and the ugly ones. Others might influence your thinking, but you have the ability to think differently. If you want to upset yourself because your parents *should* on you, go ahead. However, it's not mandatory. Where do you think you learned most of your *shoulds*? Where do you think you were taught to *should* profusely on others? And none of that "But they *shouldn't* be that way." Most likely, they were acting that way long before you were born, and they will continue to act that way long into the future. That is the way they behave. Put the focus on you, your self-talk, and the way you react to them. It might be nice if they were not that way or if they would change, but don't hold your breath waiting for a transformation. Change the way you react to them. You can also try to be somewhat tolerant; after all, they tolerated you for many years.

Start out by accepting that they are flawed and fallible humans too, and that they are the way they are. Then remind yourself that even though you don't like it, you don't *have to* upset yourself about it. Next, learn to translate their *shoulds* silently to yourself. When they tell you how you *should* raise your kids or how you *must* visit over the holidays, agree with them that you understand that they think it would be best if you raised your kids the way they prefer, but you have other preferences. Then change the subject. You have the option to simply point out that you have differences of opinions on where to spend the holidays and leave it at that.

Of course, if you're feeling lucky, you could explain to them that their *shoulds* are irrational and turn visits with them into annoying rather than enjoyable times. You can suggest they put all of the *shoulds* on a tape, which you will consider listening to when you want to get into a foul mood. They might even listen. Hell might freeze over too. You would be better off learning to translate their *shoulds* and then give them this book for their birthday or anniversary. They may read it. Again, unfortunately, hell may freeze over first and you may see flying pigs before they read it. You are not likely to change them, so consider the option to stop upsetting yourself over things you cannot control—but please buy them this book just in case! You may end up spending less and less time with them because you find it so unpleasant. By the way, there is no law that says you *must* spend time with your parents. It's a choice. What would be really annoying is if they read this book first, fall in love with it, and start practicing the hell out of it. Then they decide that they don't like spending time hanging around you and listening to you whine about your marriage and why your spouse refuses to act the way a spouse *should*.

Bosses and Coworkers
What about the boss who acts like such a jerk? Or your coworkers—you know, the people at work who gossip and complain all the time. Don't you just hate it? Or do you join them?

Of course nobody's perfect, but what a perfect place to practice your relationship skills. Yes, people are the way they are. In other words, they routinely act the way do and they typically avoid changing deeply ingrained habits. Anyone can act poorly or worse from time to time, including your boss and coworkers. If they behave poorly a lot of the time, and have a reputation for doing so, then what do you expect? Try this: The next time your boss or coworkers act like jerks, gossips, or whiners, ask yourself, "Why *shouldn't* they act that way? They've been that way ever since I've been here." The odds are, assuming your assessment was correct, that the boss is just acting like he usually acts. And believe it or not, that's the way your coworkers usually act. This situation just may be a fact of life.

Remind yourself 50 times a day that you refuse to needlessly upset yourself because you think the boss acts like a jerk or your coworkers behave inappropriately. Don't forget to take into consideration extenuating circumstances, especially if it is only a rare occurrence. Making yourself mad, sad, depressed, or any other form of upset is not likely to make bosses or coworkers behave any better. Try focusing on your job and your work. You might even try asserting yourself: "I would prefer that you don't do that [*or* act like that]," or "Please don't do that." You might decide to express your likes or dislikes. But only you can decide whether that is wise. If you do express them, do so in a reasonable way without blaming.

If you have complaints, it is usually best to offer reasonable solutions when you express them. Wait to express your opinions until you are calm, not when you're blowing off steam because you have "had it up to here." Don't forget that there may be adverse consequences to speaking up. Only you can decide if speaking up is in your best interest. Maybe you can change your focus to the reason you still work there, even if that is only for the paycheck you get. Complaining about the unfairness of it all only adds to your stress and aggravation. And where is the rule written that says it *must* always seem fair to you? Take responsibility for your choices and your happiness or lack of happiness. It is your choice to be there. Avoid playing the "I *have to* work here" card. You don't *have to* work there. It might be in your best interest to stay there at least for now, at least until you have found something else to do or some other place else to work. However, staying there is, at least for the most part, your choice.

Like you, others are flawed and fallible human beings. They are probably doing the best they can with what coping mechanisms they have. They just happen to have developed some screwed-up software and a few nutty beliefs about dealing with others. That's too bad, but it happens. Upsetting yourself about it won't change either of those things. Consider changing yourself instead.

If you decide to stay and whine for eternity about the unfairness of it all, try whining while trying to do an impression of Kermit the Frog. This will change the pitch of your whining, sound much more annoying to others, and might end up making you laugh at yourself, alleviating that exasperation that made you whine in the first place. There is nothing more grating than whining from Uranus.

CHAPTER TWELVE

Alleged Codependency

Unhealthy Love From Uranus

THE TERM *CODEPENDENCY* WAS coined to go beyond everyday unhealthy dependence. It is the worst of the worst, the tyrannical Uranian dictator of unhealthy dependencies. Codependency is essentially the common variety version of unhealthy relating that has been magnified to extremes. We would be hard pressed to find a relationship that didn't rely on dependence to some extent, to the benefit of both partners. That kind of dependence is normal give-and-take, but codependency is a form of extremely lopsided interactions between a giver and a taker in which the giver seems to typically get left holding the short end of the stick.

Do you suspect that you may be afflicted with the dreaded unhealthy kind of dependence? Have others said to you that you act like a doormat or a dishrag? Do you privately think that you are always giving and never getting? And what do you do about it if you find out that—heaven forbid—you are the poster child for unhealthy dependence?

Fear not. The solution is pretty simple. Of course, *simple* is not to be confused with *easy*. Codependency is simpler to overcome than you might think. But it isn't easy to change, because changing will require you to do some hard work to break old habits. The concepts behind that hard work are simple, however, and you are holding them in your hand this very second. Yes, you are holding the treatment manual for overcoming unhealthy dependence. The skills provided in *We Are All From Uranus* are the basic fundamental skills of healthy independence. And guess what—healthy independence is generally incompatible with unhealthy dependence. As you apply the techniques in this book, you will begin to extinguish your unhealthy thinking and behaving from Uranus. You will be replacing them with your newfound healthy attitude.

How Do I Know If I Have Contracted This Dreaded Condition?

There are several significant features of unhealthy dependence: self-deprivation, suffering, self-sacrifice, feelings of unworthiness, feelings of being unlovable, the *need* for approval, fear of abandonment, and chronic guilt. One of the most of significant patterns of codependency is the belief that "to prove my worthiness, I *must* sacrifice myself forever to make everyone in my environment happy." This typically leads to ignoring your own wants and desires, not setting reasonable boundaries with others, and feeling dissatisfied and guilty. You feel uncomfortable unless you are forever sacrificing yourself. Typically this eventually leads to pent-up feelings of anger because you constantly sacrifice and do countless good deeds for others but think that you get nothing in return: "When I screw up and fail to provide happiness to all, all I get is those people constantly putting me down."

Ironically, there are incredibly strong fail-safe mechanisms in place that inhibit changing: fear of abandonment, fear of the unknown, and fear of incredible guilt. The triple whammy! "If I am abandoned, I will be alone and will never survive the pain of grieving. I am so unworthy and unlovable. I will grieve and be alone forever because no one else could ever love a miserable and lowly person like me. It is very scary out in the world. When I think about it, I feel incredibly anxious. I could never take care of myself all alone. When I am here, at least things are familiar and predictable. I feel so guilty and miserable when I dare to think of myself and try to put myself first. I don't deserve it. I am failing in my sacred mission to sacrifice myself for others for all eternity. I feel so selfish when I even consider what I want. I *shouldn't* focus on myself. I *shouldn't* put myself first. I am such a martyr, and what kind of decent martyr would ever think of putting themselves first? Oh no—I'm even a lousy martyr. I *should* feel so guilty."

You can see why changing requires focusing on you, but focusing on yourself creates incredible guilt that seems to prevent escape. You have been telling yourself for a very long time that you *shouldn't* put yourself first. You do remember that when you *should* on yourself, you feel guiltier and guiltier as you fan the flames with more *shoulds*? The intensity of the guilt you create is so strong that there is a tendency to abandon focusing on yourself. And you return your focus to others, which then relieves the feelings of guilt. This is similar to choosing to stay in a bad relationship to avoid the painful grief of leaving. Most people don't push to the head of the line in order to volunteer to leave.

In this case, you are choosing to stay in an unhealthy relationship...with yourself. It may be necessary to struggle through a lot of painful feelings in order to be successful. This is a pretty tall order. If you decide to escape your unhealthy beliefs, you will likely succumb to confronting and dealing with all of those unpleasant feelings at one time: grief, anxiety, and guilt. It is all too easy to stay with the attraction and comfort of familiarity. It is no wonder that breaking the shackles and escaping the pull of unhealthy dependence is so difficult—it has as strong a pull as gravity. Working on healthy relationship skills requires a lifelong effort. Be patient and realize that these traits have been there for a long time and can't be changed overnight. But if you do not actively choose to work on making healthy changes, you are passively choosing to remain in an unhealthy state of dependence. Try not to forget that even the smallest of changes add up over time.

How Did I Learn to Be Such an Expert Martyr?
Where do people learn to be martyrs, which involves incredibly warped thinking? Unfortunately, it is all too common for people to think this way, and the brain we inherit likely has something to do with it. Even though it occurs in males and females, unhealthy dependence is especially common in women, who historically were taught to be the ones responsible for caregiving. Cinderella, Snow White, and the rest of the gang were told that Prince Charming is out there somewhere and that if they snatch him up once he comes along and take care of his every *need*, they will live happily ever after. This is the formula for happiness we have been taught, and as for deviating from it...well, we all know what happened to Cinderella's evil stepsisters and Snow White's wicked stepmother. If you were taught to think this way, you were convinced that your worth comes from taking care of others—a spouse, children, and so on. To be considered worthwhile, you were taught that you *should* make others happy. That you *should* eliminate any unpleasantness from others' lives. That you *must* avoid all conflicts and arguments, because you *need* and *must* have others' love and approval. You learned that you *should* have a perfectly conflict-free place to call home. In fact, you learned that it is your responsibility to ensure that

all of these requirements are met. And that if you don't provide that, you are one hell of a loser.

You watched your parents and the rest of your world and received, or perceived, message after message that you are responsible for other people's feelings. You *should* and *must* make them happy, and you *should* not and *must* not make them angry or upset. The message was: "This is so important that you *should* and *must* put yourself last." If you do not, you are selfish. If there are scraps, you can have them. To do it any other way would only prove that you are self-centered and selfish. "You *must*! You *should*!" When you didn't have the approval of your parents, you might have felt the pain of rejection, and whether that rejection was real or imagined, it still doesn't feel good even now. By this point in your life, you *must* avoid rejection at all costs. You *must* do for others.

Can you see why it is not easy to get rid of unhealthy dependence? The unhealthy rules you have learned preclude the first step: putting yourself first, leveling the playing field, and elevating yourself to the realistic position of being a *worthy and flawed and fallible human being*. Every time you try to get better, you create instant guilt by thinking, "I *shouldn't* put myself first. I am only being selfish. Selfishness is terrible and *must* be avoided. What will they think of me? I will be exiled to eternal suffering in the valley of the damned." Look, we are not trying to tell you not to do things for others. It is okay to do for others, and at times it may be in your best interest to do so. Giving is a very important part of relationships and frequently very enjoyable. But don't forget that it is also okay for others to do for you. Reciprocating is also an important part of most any healthy relationship.

Also, consider that even though it may not feel like it, you do for others by choice. You don't do it because of some unhealthy *should* so that you can prove your worth as a person, or so you can somehow fulfill your *need* to be approved of by your partner. It is your perceived *need*. It is up to you to work on changing it to a preference. Wanting to do for others or preferring to do for others is one thing. *Needing* to is entirely different. Guess which is healthier?

If you want to do things for others, it is important that you also do things for yourself. If you fail to take care of yourself and your own happiness, you will likely be less proficient in taking care of or helping others. You will inadvertently be passing the curse of Uranus onto another generation.

If you decide to fight this unhealthy habit of dependence, you will feel very uncomfortable doing something that is so unusual and out of character. You probably will feel very unsure of yourself and worry excessively. That's why people who do experiment with healthier approaches often quickly abandon them. It feels uncomfortable. The head (cerebral cortex) knows what to do, but the heart (limbic system) feels peculiar, anxious, or guilty. If you follow your "heart," it might feel better, but if you don't make an effort to overcome unhealthy relationship habits, it is unlikely that any meaningful change will take place. And yes, it may take great effort because you have learned these habits from Uranus, where force of habit is one of the strongest forces in the universe, especially when it comes to our fallibility.

Look carefully at yourself and listen to your self-talk to find what you are telling yourself to encourage this gut feeling. Are you telling yourself something healthy, or something unhealthy instead? Evaluate your thoughts as well as your choices, and the outcomes that are in your best interest. We suggest you follow your head and think about effective behavior. Work to act on thoughtful choices rather than being a slave to your feelings like the majority of the human race. Don't forget, *gut = limbic system*, just as *heart = limbic system*. If you have forgotten where feelings come from, go back and reread Chapter 4 ("Where Do

Feelings Come From—Mars? Venus? Uranus?") and Chapter 5 ("Responsibility Versus Influence"). If you continue to work on changing for the better in spite of the funny feelings, the gut and heart will eventually have an opportunity catch up. You will eventually have developed a new habit, a healthier habit. And you will feel much more comfortable with the new behaviors and attitudes. You will also gain the potential for healthier results in your relationships.

Work on learning to take care of yourself and your happiness. You are an important person. If you want to be happy, it is up to you to make your own happiness and not depend on others to make you happy. Don't forget that there is no law of the universe that everyone *must* like you or love you, or that you *must* be the most wonderful person who has ever lived, someone who "deserves" eternal happiness. Sometimes others will agree with you and like you, and sometimes they won't. Sometimes others will even upset themselves about you. Sometimes others may not like you at all. This is part of life. You may not like it, but you are responsible for your own happiness, and with some work and all other things being equal, you can learn to accept reality and deal with it. On the next page is a brief review of how the points previously mentioned are incompatible with unhealthy dependence.

Sometimes unhealthy dependence predisposes a person to stay in abusive relationships. Frequently, people who find themselves in this position of abuse have been exposed to some abuse in their past: mental, physical, or sexual. If you are currently in an abusive relationship, it usually reinforces your belief that you are worthless. If you find yourself in an abusive situation, keep yourself safe and get help when it does not endanger you. Seek out a therapist, psychologist, social worker, abuse-counseling service, abuse hotline, or some other source of support. Abusive situations can be very difficult for people to leave. Try not to let your past, if you were abused, continue in the present. Try not to let feelings of embarrassment, shame, or guilt keep you in an abusive relationship. Get help and remember to stay safe!

Unhealthy Dependence	1 Wormhood, unworthiness, poor self-acceptance: "I am not a good person unless I prove it by taking care of everyone else." 2 Rigidity; *should, must, have to*: "I *must* take care of everyone." 3 Responsibility for everyone: "I am responsible for others' feelings. I *must* make them happy." 4 Need for others' approval: "I can't stand it if someone is unhappy with me."
Healthy Independence	1 Self-acceptance: "I can accept myself even if they do not accept me." 2 Flexibility: "I can do for others if I choose to." 3 Responsibility for the self: "I am responsible for my feelings. It is okay to do for others, but they are responsible for their own happiness." 4 Independence: "I can stand it, but I don't like it when others are unhappy with me."

CHAPTER THIRTEEN

Epilogue

This was it, the moment when everything clicked. The pieces all fit together, and Barbara knew without a doubt what she wanted. Paul had surprised her with a romantic dinner, complete with candlelight and roses. As they slowly undressed each other, she could feel her euphoria rising with each drugging kiss, each searing caress. With every heated look from him, she felt beautiful, wanted, desired. The soft flickering light from the vanilla-scented candles created a dreamy atmosphere, enhancing each gentle touch and whispered endearment in the glowing half-light. She loved him. She could feel it in every fiber of her being. As he pulled back, looking at her with tenderness and longing, she knew he felt the same way; she saw it deep within his eyes. It wasn't just this intense physical connection, the sparks flying between them, but his tenderness, the way he listened to her every word, the way he comforted her when she hurt. She felt a strong primal desire to do all that was in her power to make this strong, passionate, caring man as happy as he made her.

She loved making the extra effort to do all the little things that Paul appreciated, those small special details like having a cup of coffee ready for him when he woke up, as he claimed he felt comatose until he had that first revitalizing cup. He always smiled at her after he took his first sip, knowing she'd taken the time to pay attention to that little detail that made waking up early bearable for him. He was her perfect match, always working to be an equal partner in their relationship, always working to make it so successful. Their passion still burned bright. When they kissed, the rest of the world and its trials disappeared.

Barbara knows Paul wants her because he still tells her so every day. After all their years together, his passion still hasn't diminished. She loves being with him and still can't seem to keep her hands off him. Even when he has to travel for business and she feels the emptiness of their separation, she reminds herself that when he returns, she'll get to welcome him home with loving arms and a warm kiss.

Barbara knows what she wants. Paul is the only man, partner, and lover for her. She could never find a replacement for the kind of wonderful, dedicated, and caring partner that Paul is. Together they make the perfect couple, like two peas in a pod, and hand in hand they go. Their relationship is thriving and strong. At this thought, Barbara smiles up at Paul, awash in happiness and the comforting sense of security she feels in his arms and in their relationship. As they come together, she knows that he is the only man she wants to be with, love, and cherish. As they celebrate their love, Barbara hopes and believes that she will be with Paul for a very, very long time.

Paul can't get enough of Barbara either. He had planned this night with care, wanting to make her feel special, wanting to show her how intensely he desired and cherished her. Her satiny skin begs for his touch. Her own unique scent tugs at him, telling him that this is the woman he wants and loves; all others pale in her light. It's her smile, the look she gives him when he reveals the bedroom that he'd transformed into a warm love nest, the soft sigh she makes as he kisses her neck. Barbara

EPILOGUE

gazes lovingly at him, caressing his face tenderly, and Paul knows from the depth of his very being that she cares for him as strongly as he cares for her. She is generous with her affection, not just when they're in the bedroom but all the time he is around. Her touch and the sight of her stir him as deeply as when he had first laid eyes on her and felt his heart skip a beat.

He loves doing things for her, paying attention to all the little details that he is sure will make her happy, and he basks in her smile of delight when he brings her breakfast in bed, rubs her shoulders, or gives her a foot massage. She still kisses him as if the rest of the world has ceased to exist, and tells him every day how she can hardly wait to touch him. She teases that she still can't seem to keep her hands to herself around him. Paul replies with a grin that he has the same problem when she's in the room. When they are apart, he eagerly looks forward to returning and taking her in his arms as soon as he walks through the door. She is there for him when the chips are down, supporting and completing him. They are two halves of one whole. Barbara is the only one for Paul. She is irreplaceable in his eyes, and he works hard to be the best possible partner for her as well. He knows as he holds her in his arms that she is the only woman he wants to be with, love, and cherish. Love fills him when Barbara lays her head on his chest, curling into his embrace, and Paul hopes and believes that he will be with her for a very, very long time.

A very, very long time. As long as possible. Partners. Together.

Where did all that love come from? And why had it gone *poof* by the time we first met Paul and Barbara? Did it vanish into thin air? But if it once more looks as good as it did at the start of their relationship, perhaps they've done something to change their previously gloomy fate.

Sure, things change. Reality can intrude on passion. Money can go for diapers rather than playtime. Good behavior and a desire to please can be replaced by bad moods, stress, sweat pants, and a five o'clock shadow. The person who inspires passion and happiness can disappear, replaced by someone who generates an aura of annoyance. But does this *have to* happen? Is there any hope? How can it possibly be prevented?

Here's how: The prince and princess got married, bought this book, read this book very thoroughly, and agreed to work on healthy ways of relating in order to maximize the happiness and health of their relationship for as long as possible.

Well, We Were All From Uranus
It's not the subtle differences between men and women that are the main difficulties for poor relationships. It is unhealthy thinking from Uranus, unhealthy thinking that requires work and effort to conquer. Poor relationships are the result of lifelong unhealthy habits. Fortunately, unhealthy habits can be overcome by replacing them with healthy relationship skills. Both men and woman can unlearn their unhealthy beliefs and behaviors, regardless of how they acquired them, and replace them with healthy ones. This is the key to relationship success.

Remember, on Uranus as men and women emerged from caves, their primitive state of knowledge about relationships was passed down from generation to generation. The current unhealthy fundamentals of relating originate from the dark ages, characterized by superstitions and irrational fear; belief in magic, witchcraft, and fantastical creatures; ignorance; and fantasies about fairy-tale relationships. But these were people whose relationship skills resulted in the Inquisition—not exactly the best example to follow. The people on Uranus unwittingly continue to use these primitive ways of relating that they inherited from childhood. Never questioning, they refuse to challenge or change those unhealthy beliefs even as their relationships aimlessly sputter and spontaneously self-destruct.

EPILOGUE

Perhaps now, after reading this book, they recognize that denying the folly of their ways can only perpetuate their misery. They may prefer not to ignorantly rationalize, justify, signify, dignify, and downright lie their way through relationships. They may see the benefits of enhancing their flexibility and accepting that they are mere flawed and fallible human beings. They may be willing to take responsibility for their own thoughts, feelings, and behaviors. They may understand that they don't know everything there is to know about relationships and are perhaps now willing to ask questions, to search, learn, and practice in order to improve themselves. They may realize that working toward improving relationship skills is a goal; it's not an end but a way of life. Hmmm, they *are* starting to get it. It's about relating—healthy relations.

But they can be aware of the struggle that continues. It's easy for most people to enjoy the good times, but it takes healthy skills to deal with the bad times. It will be the disagreements, the dislikes, and the arguments that will be hardest to overcome. Most every relationship has them. How you handle them will be the key to your success. The good times are easy; the bad times are difficult.

There's an old story about a guy in New York City who asked a passerby, "How do you get to Carnegie Hall?" The passerby replied, "Practice!" If you practice, you will amaze yourself and your friends with your new skills. You will be on the road to having better relationships. You will increase the chances that your life will be filled with more happiness and less grumbling, and you won't be accused of thinking from Uranus. Stop to enjoy your relationships and enjoy your journey. It's simple, but it's not easy!

APPENDIX I

Quick Reference

Healthy Rules

1 **Self-acceptance:** We are all flawed and fallible.
   a Work to eliminate the habit of beating yourself up. Learn from your mistakes.
   b Work to eliminate any kind of rating or labeling of yourself or others. See yourself for what you are: an imperfect human being.
   c Accept yourself even with your flaws and recognize that you will either work hard to reduce your flaws or work hard to cope with them.
2 **Flexibility**: Work to increase your flexibility and to reduce your rigidity.
   a Increase your preferential thinking by using words such as *want, wish,* and *prefer.*
   b Decrease your rigid demanding thinking by avoiding words such as *should, must, have to, need to.*
3 **Responsibility:** Take personal responsibility for your own feelings, thoughts, and behaviors. You are responsible for your own happiness, and you are responsible for your own

upset. Don't blame others for it. See your life as a series of choices, not as things you "*have to*" do. Take responsibility for your choices. See the choices as yours and don't blame them on others. Rate your choices as healthy ones or unhealthy ones.

Negotiating and compromising are important components of a successful relationship. These can be enhanced by

1. **Accurate communication:** Say what you mean and mean what you say.
2. **Asking:** Ask if you want something. Don't expect others to read your mind and don't deprive them of the opportunity to tell you no.
3. **Positive reinforcement:** Reward in some positive fashion the behaviors or traits that you like in your partner. Give most of your attention to the things they do that you like.
4. **Decreasing punishment:** Pay less attention to your partner's behaviors that you don't like. Ignore them completely if possible. When you do respond to them, remember to focus more on the behaviors and traits that you like than on the ones you don't like.

Criticism—that is, healthy criticism—is important.

1. **Present criticism as your opinion:** If you do have a criticism, present it as your opinion of something that you do not like. Refrain from discussing it as though it were a universal rule that *must* be followed no matter what, as though only a blithering idiot would fail to see that and continue to engage in the disliked behavior after it was pointed out to them for the one zillionth time.
2. **Avoid blaming:** Blaming only gets you off track and leads to a contest of who is the good guy and who is the bad guy.

Is it really any wonder that people get defensive when they get blamed?

3 **Use "I" statements rather than "you" statements:** Make sure you use a lot of them. "You" leads to accusations, blaming, and defensiveness.
4 **Translate the criticism you receive from others:** When they call you stupid, meaning that you are a stupid person, translate it to a behavior or trait. "Yes, sometimes I do stupid things." It is most likely that you do or have done stupid things. That doesn't make you a stupid person. It just makes you a person who acted stupidly.

In choosing your partner, look for a preponderance of these positive traits:

1 Compatibility
2 A sense of humor
3 Reliability and straightforwardness: They mean what they say and do what they say they will do.
4 Flexibility
5 Self-responsibility
6 A willingness to communicate their likes and dislikes
7 A willingness to handle dislikes reasonably

In choosing your partner, beware these negative traits and behaviors:

1 Giving you a lot of gifts and presents
2 Saying they "love" you even when they haven't had the time to get to know you
3 Incompatibilities: Do not overlook things that annoy you. Those cutesy habits will get to you months from now.

4 No sense of humor: Think about actually living with it every day, and how that might eventually make you feel. Do this rather than trying to ignore it and explain away its lack to your friends.
5 Distance, unreliability, and a tendency to disregard what you think is important
6 Incompatibility: If you think that you *have to* work too hard to keep the relationship alive, perhaps you are correct. Maybe it really is one-sided and you really are working too hard. Maybe it's time to suck it up and move on.
7 Rigidity, being demanding, being overly jealous: These behaviors indicate a serious lack of understanding about dependence on their part—and on your part if you go along with it. They may be getting their self-worth from their relationship with you. You may think at first that it is great that someone "can't live without you." But that's a dangerous statement, not a romantic one. Don't you watch those stalker movies?
8 Blaming others: People who blame their troubles on others lack the insight to really make a change in their life. Beware if you are the person whom your partner expects to make them happy or the person they blame if they are unhappy. Isn't that one of the common denominators in abusive relationships? "If you would only do what I tell you to, I wouldn't *have to* yell at you and toss you around. You drive me crazy. You make me mad. You could make me so happy if you would just..."
9 Avoidance of communication: Unless you have graduated from Madame X's School of Mind Reading, how are you supposed to know what your partner wants if they won't tell you? Some people believe you will know because you are in love with them. "If you really loved me, you would know what I like."

Daily reminder

Consider changing the things you can change and ignoring the things you can't change. Try to think rationally enough to know the difference and avoid upsetting yourself needlessly in the meantime.

How to change your thinking

1 **Identify what you are telling yourself:** It is usually a healthy idea to write it down. Look for the healthy thoughts and ideas and also pinpoint the unhealthy ones.
2 **Challenge your unhealthy thinking:** This is the part that is causing your upset. Be sure to challenge it with gusto. Do it forcefully and be prepared to put in a good deal of practice.
3 **Replace your unhealthy thinking with healthy thinking:** For example, "I *should* have known better" becomes "I wish I had known better" or "It would have been better if I had known then what I know now. But I didn't know, and that doesn't make me a bad person. It only proves that I am flawed and fallible like the rest of us humans." Then practice, practice, practice!

APPENDIX II

Exercises

Exercise 3-1: Decreasing Shoulds and Increasing Preferential Thinking

Use the skills that you learned in Chapter 3 ("The *Should-ectomy* . . . Exorcising the *Shoulds* From Uranus") to identify your *shoulds* and change them to preferential thinking. In the table on the following page, write out your *shoulds* in the left column and then rewrite them in the right column using preferential thinking.

Shoulds	Preferential Thinking
1 I *should* have…	1 It would have been better if I had…
2 You *shouldn't* do that.	2 I would prefer you don't do that.
3	3

Exercise 5-1: Self-Talk and Feelings

This is an exercise to demonstrate how thoughts cause or influence feelings and to help you identify your self-talk. Pick a past instance when you felt angry, sad, happy, or guilty. Identify what you were telling yourself and write it in the boxes below.

Feelings	*Self-Talk*
Angry	Identify the self-talk that makes you feel angry: **Example:** "They *shouldn't* have done that."
Sad	Identify the self-talk that makes you feel sad: **Example:** "I will be alone forever."
Happy	Identify the self-talk that makes you feel happy: **Example:** "It was so wonderful for my husband to bring me flowers."
Guilty	Identify the self-talk that makes you feel guilty: **Example:** "I *shouldn't* have done that."

Practicing the following exercise will prepare you for Exercise 5-2. Choose an instance when you were really upset, and then follow these steps:

1. Write down how you felt.
2. Write down what you were telling yourself.
3. Now write down something healthier you can tell yourself as a substitute.
4. Now, sit down and try to make yourself cry.
5. Repeat steps 1 and 2.
6. Now try to make yourself smile.
7. Repeat steps 1 and 2.
8. Do you see the relationship between thoughts that make you tearful and thoughts that make you smile? Do you see what happens when you change your thoughts? Keep practicing this one until you get it.

Exercise 5-2: Changing Unhealthy Thinking

Changing your unhealthy thinking is as easy as one, two, three.... Okay, it's simple but not easy. There are three steps to changing unhealthy self-talk. At first, you'll find it easier if you write these out. With practice, you will become better and better at doing them in your head.

Step	Example	Practice
1 **Identify** the unhealthy thought.	"I *shouldn't* have done that."	**Identify**
2 **Challenge** the unhealthy thought.	"*Shoulds* are unhealthy and really don't exist. They are only irrational rules that I have learned. When I tell myself I *shouldn't* do something, I feel guilty."	**Challenge**
3 **Replace** with a healthy thought.	"I made a mistake. I would prefer not to make mistakes. But I am human. That doesn't mean I am a bad person. It only proves I am a flawed and fallible human being. I will try to turn it into something positive and learn from my mistake."	**Replace**

Exercise 8-1: Mutual, Bilateral, Simultaneous, Parallel Practice Application for Conflict Resolution

This is an exercise that helps each partner take responsibility for their thoughts, feelings, and behaviors. Both you and your partner write down your perspective on a given conflict.

Me	*Partner*
1 What happened?	1 What happened?
2 What did I tell myself about it to cause upset?	2 What did I tell myself about it to cause upset?
3 How did I make myself feel?	3 How did I make myself feel?
4 What did I do when I was upset?	4 What did I do when I was upset?

Me	Partner
5 How would I prefer to think, feel, and behave?	5 How would I prefer to think, feel, and behave?

Repeat the exercise, this time replacing steps 2 and 4 with more reasonable thoughts and behaviors that will help you toward achieving the outcomes you desire. Then practice, practice, practice!

APPENDIX III

Recommended Reading

Beck, A.T. (1999). *Prisoners of Hate: The Cognitive Basis of Anger, Hostility, and Violence.* New York, NY: HarperCollins.

Bloom, P. (2002). *How Children Learn the Meaning of Words.* Cambridge, MA: MIT Press.

Brown, T.E. (2005). *Attention Deficit Disorder: The Unfocused Mind in Children and Adults.* New Haven, CT: Yale University Press.

Browne, M.N., & Keeley, S.M. (2007). *Asking the Right Questions: A Guide to Critical Thinking* (8th ed.). NJ: Pearson Prentice Hall, NJ: Pearson Prentice Hall.

Chabris, C., & Simons, D. (2010). *The Invisible Gorilla: And Other Ways Our Intuitions Deceive Us.* New York, NY: Crown Publishers.

Ellis, A., & Harper R.A. (1997). *A Guide to Rational Living* (3rd ed.; original work published 1976). North Hollywood, CA: Melvin Powers Wilshire Book Company.

Ellis, A. (2001). *Overcoming Destructive Beliefs, Feelings, and Behaviors.* Amherst, NY: Prometheus Books.

Gilovich, T. (1991). *How We Know What Isn't So: The Fallibility of Human Reason in Everyday Life.* New York, NY: Free Press.

Jones, M.D. (1998). *The Thinker's Toolkit: 14 Powerful Techniques for Problem Solving*. New York, NY: Three Rivers Press.

Kahneman, D. (2011). *Thinking, Fast and Slow*. New York, NY: Farrar, Straus & Giroux.

Kida, T.E. (2006). *Don't Believe Everything You Think: The 6 Basic Mistakes We Make in Thinking*. Amherst, NY: Prometheus Books.

LeDoux, J.E. (2002). *Synaptic Self: How Our Brains Become Who We Are*. New York, NY: Russell Sage Foundation.